Trailblazers

Jamestown's Critical Reading Program

Trailblazers

15 Dramatic Stories of Adventure and Exploration—with Exercises for Developing Reading Comprehension and Critical Thinking Skills

McGraw Hill Education

Bothell, WA • Chicago, IL • Columbus, OH • New York, NY

mheonline.com

 **Education**

Send all inquiries to:
McGraw-Hill Education
130 E. Randolph, Suite 400
Chicago, IL 60601

ISBN: 978-0-07-659070-4
MHID: 0-07-659070-4

Printed in the United States of America.

3 4 5 6 7 8 9 QDB 15 14 13 12

The **McGraw·Hill** Companies

Contents

Unit Three

To the Student

A trailblazer is a seeker, an explorer looking for a path to a new place, a better place, sometimes even a place no one else can believe truly exists. In a way, every person is a trailblazer, exploring his or her unique path through life. Any goal you seek is a destination. Every goal is a possible adventure—your *own* adventure—and the path from the beginning to the end depends on you and your ability to visualize the result and then go for it.

Trailblazers never know for certain just what their journey will reveal. After all, who can really predict the future? But as the poet T. S. Eliot once said, "Only those who will risk going too far can possibly find out how far they can go." Any true adventure or exploration begins with a willingness to go ahead, to take a risk despite the possibility of failure. Forward motion comes with throwing off the fear of failure and making an investment in reaching the goal.

Each lesson in this book tells the story of someone who set out to blaze a trail from Here to There and accepted the risks and challenges to make it happen. Some of the trailblazers you will read about look for adventure and the thrill of discovery. They want to dive the deepest, climb the highest, or go to the most remote places. Others are driven to test themselves or to prove a point by putting enormous effort behind their beliefs. Still others long to shake off the natural limitations that hold most human beings back.

As you read and enjoy the articles, you will also develop your reading skills. *Trailblazers* is for students who already read fairly well but who want to read faster and to increase their understanding of what they read. If you complete the 15 lessons—reading the articles and completing the exercises—you will surely increase your reading speed and improve your reading comprehension and critical thinking skills. Also, because these exercises include items of the types often found on state and national tests, you will find that learning how to complete them will prepare you for tests you may have to take in the future.

How to Use This Book

About the Book. *Trailblazers* contains three units, each of which includes five lessons. Each lesson begins with an article about a unique event, person, or group. The article is followed by a group of four reading comprehension exercises and a set of three critical thinking exercises. The reading comprehension exercises will help you understand the article. The critical thinking exercises will help you think about what you have read and how it relates to your own experience.

At the end of each lesson, you will also have the opportunity to give your personal response to some aspect of the article and then to assess how well you understood what you read.

The Sample Lesson. Working through the sample lesson, the first lesson in the book, with your class or group will demonstrate how a lesson is organized. The sample lesson explains how to complete the exercises and score your answers. The correct answers for the sample exercises and sample scores are printed in lighter type. In some cases, explanations of the correct answers are given. The explanations will help you understand how to think through these question types.

If you have any questions about how to complete the exercises or score them, this is the time to get the answers.

Working Through Each Lesson. Begin each lesson by looking at the photographs and reading the captions. Before you read, predict what you think the article will be about. Then read the article.

Sometimes your teacher may decide to time your reading. Timing helps you keep track of and increase your reading speed. If you have been timed, enter your reading time in the box at the end of the article. Then use the Words-per-Minute Table to find your reading speed, and record your speed on the Reading Speed graph at the end of the unit.

Next, complete the Reading Comprehension and Critical Thinking exercises. The directions for each exercise will tell you how to mark your answers. When you have finished all four Reading Comprehension exercises, use the answer key provided by your teacher to check your work. Follow the directions after each exercise to find your score. Record your Reading Comprehension scores on the graph at the end of each unit. Then check your answers to the Author's Approach, Summarizing and Paraphrasing, and Critical Thinking exercises. Fill in the Critical Thinking chart at the end of each unit with your evaluation of your work and comments about your progress.

At the end of each unit you will also complete a Compare and Contrast chart. The completed chart will help you see what the articles have in common. It will also give you an opportunity to explore your own ideas about Trailblazers—who they are, what they are looking for, and what they will do to find it.

On Thin Ice

A team of sled dogs can pull hundreds of pounds for several hours over frozen terrain.

"Life can be pretty miserable: You're eating disgusting freeze-dried food every night, your tent's being pounded by blizzards, you have ice building up inside your thermal underwear. . . ." Why on earth would adventurer Tom Avery cause himself such misery on purpose? He did it to make a point. Avery was the leader of a 2005 North Pole expedition. The sole purpose of Avery's journey was to show that Robert E. Peary actually could have done what he said he did. In 1909 Peary claimed that he, along with his assistant Matthew Henson and four Inuit men, were the first explorers to reach the North Pole. Peary asserted that they accomplished this feat in just 37 days by traveling on foot 413 nautical miles with sled dogs. Was such an achievement possible in so short a time? Tom Avery was hoping to find out.

2   Controversy has raged within the polar explorer community ever since Peary made his claim to the North Pole. Many experts have expressed doubt that Peary and Henson ever made it to the North Pole at all, but especially not in just 37 days. These experts point out several inconsistent entries in Peary's notes. They also wonder how Peary's team overcame the seemingly insurmountable obstacle of crossing the frozen Arctic Ocean. According to these experts, the first explorer who reached the North Pole was Sir Wally Herbert, who got there on foot in 1969. Herbert wrote a book in 1989 in which he analyzes Peary's expedition. From his calculations, Herbert concludes that Peary could not have reached the North Pole. According to Herbert, it was he, and not Peary, who was the first explorer to reach the North Pole.

3   Tom Avery was the perfect candidate to test Peary's claim. Avery had previously journeyed to the South Pole. He had also been on several major mountaineering expeditions. If he could follow Peary's route and arrive at the North Pole in just 37 days, it would add evidence to prove that Peary was telling the truth. At the very least it would keep the possibility alive.

4   In planning the trip, Avery duplicated Peary's equipment as closely as possible. He used the same number and breed of sled dogs. He made sure each team of dogs consisted of one female and seven males, just as Peary had done. The two 11-foot-long sleds were built to the same specifications as Peary's sleds. They too were made from lengths of Canadian spruce lashed together

Tom Avery hoped to prove that Robert Peary could have reached the North Pole in just 37 days.

with rope, with no screws or nails so the sleds would not catch on the ice. In addition, Avery and his four teammates—Matty McNair, Andrew Gerber, George Wells, and Hugh Dale-Harris—plotted out the exact same route that Peary and Henson had taken nearly 100 years earlier.

5 Avery and his team faced formidable challenges crossing the Arctic Ocean in a time of increased global warming. In 2005 and today, the frozen Arctic Ocean is much different than it was in 1909. First of all, there is far more open water. Second, the ice pack is thinner, making it more likely to give way under the explorers' weight. Finally, the pressure ridges—those towering walls of ice formed when one sheet of ice pushes into another—are more numerous and less stable than previously, even though they are smaller. In some ways, then, Avery faced even more obstacles than Peary did. However, the Arctic Ocean is a dangerous place to be in any time period. "It's not an exaggeration to say that as soon as you set foot on the ice, the place is trying to kill you," says Avery.

6 Part of the danger comes from the extreme cold and darkness. To travel in relative safety across the ice, explorers need to begin during the Arctic winter, which is early March. At this time of the year, the sun barely makes an appearance before sinking beneath the horizon again. The temperature can drop as low as 40 degrees below zero Fahrenheit. As Avery says, "Humans aren't designed to survive those temperatures; your body just shuts down."

7 Another problem comes from the staggeringly high number of calories needed to fuel the human body on such a journey. Because of the extreme effort of traveling across the ice pack, each member of Avery's team was using up to 10,000 calories a day. They ate all the high-energy foods they could. Their breakfasts typically consisted of granola with powdered milk, lots of sugar, and hot chocolate. During the day, they chowed down on dried fruit, nuts, cheese, salami, fudge, and biscuits. In the evening, they boiled a freeze-dried meal. In addition, the team supplemented everything with butter, butter, and more butter. Near the end of their journey, they were eating solid sticks of butter, because pure butter has more calories per gram than almost any other type of food. Even with all this food, Avery and the others were taking in only 6,500 to 7,000 calories a day. So as Avery reported, "You're effectively starving yourself."

8 As the days passed, Avery was often in despair over making it to the North Pole in time to match Peary's record. On Day 35, and time running out, they came to a section of ice they were not sure would hold them. As they attempted to cross, one team of dogs suddenly crashed through the ice and tumbled into the icy water. Luckily, the combination of the dogs' weight and their frenetic swimming and groping did not pull the sled in behind them. Avery and his crew desperately coaxed the dogs back to solid ice, and the dogs managed to scramble out of the water. A little bit later,

the group found some thicker ice, and they were able to continue on their way.

9 At last, with only a few hours to spare, Avery and his team reached the North Pole. Counting down the last 60 feet on the Global Positioning System (GPS), they walked side-by-side to the top of the world. Their time was 36 days, 22 hours, and 11 minutes. This was roughly five hours *faster* than Robert Peary's total time.

10 Tom Avery acknowledges that his North Pole expedition did not prove Peary and Henson reached the Pole. He only showed that they might have reached it—that it was possible. But that was a huge accomplishment all by itself. "If we've helped to get people talking about Peary and Henson again, and if the world now sees their achievement in a more positive light than they did before . . ." says Avery. "That's all I really want." ✳

If you have been timed while reading this article, enter your reading time below. Then turn to the Words-per-Minute Table on page 55 and look up your reading speed (words per minute). Enter your reading speed on the graph on page 56.

Reading Time: Sample Lesson

_____ : _____
Minutes   Seconds

A Finding the Main Idea

One statement below expresses the main idea of the article. One statement is too general, or too broad. The other statement explains only part of the article; it is too narrow. Label the statements using the following key:

M—Main Idea **B—Too Broad** **N—Too Narrow**

_B_ 1. Adventurer Tom Avery and his team were able to re-create the amazing feat of Robert Peary and Matthew Henson, which has been the subject of controversy for years. [This statement is true, but it is *too broad*. It does not tell what Peary and Henson did or why there is controversy about it.]

_N_ 2. For his 2005 journey, adventurer Tom Avery duplicated the equipment that Peary and Henson had used to reach the North Pole in 1909. [This statement is true, but it is *too narrow*. This statement provides only a few details about Avery's feat.]

_M_ 3. In 2005 adventurer Tom Avery and his team re-created the expedition of Robert Peary and his assistant Matthew Henson, proving that they could have walked to the North Pole in 37 days, a claim that some experts had doubted. [This statement is the *main idea*. It tells you that the article describes the reason for the expedition and its outcome.]

_15_ Score 15 points for a correct M answer.

_10_ Score 5 points for each correct B or N answer.

_25_ **Total Score**: Finding the Main Idea

B Recalling Facts

How well do you remember the facts in the article? Put an X in the box next to the answer that correctly completes each statement about the article.

1. The man who walked to the North Pole in 1969 was
   ☐ a. Tom Avery.
   ☐ b. Robert Peary.
   ☒ c. Wally Herbert.

2. For Avery's expedition, the sleds were made of
   ☐ a. lightweight aluminum.
   ☒ b. Canadian spruce wood.
   ☐ c. strong, molded plastic.

3. Temperatures near the North Pole in March can drop to
   ☒ a. 40 degrees below zero.
   ☐ b. 80 degrees below zero.
   ☐ c. 100 degrees below zero.

4. To keep up their energy on the trip, Avery's team ate
   ☒ a. lots of butter.
   ☐ b. fresh vegetables every day.
   ☐ c. sugar-free and fat-free snacks.

5. Completing the journey took Avery and his team
   ☐ a. just nine hours more than Peary took.
   ☐ b. exactly the same amount of time as Peary took.
   ☒ c. five hours fewer than Peary took.

Score 5 points for each correct answer.

_25_ **Total Score**: Recalling Facts

C Making Inferences

When you combine your own experiences and information from a text to draw a conclusion that is not directly stated in that text, you are making an inference. Below are five statements that may or may not be inferences based on information in the article. Label the statements using the following key:

C—Correct Inference   **F—Faulty Inference**

__C__ 1. Tom Avery respected Peary and Henson and their team. [This is a *correct* inference. Avery said he wanted Peary and Henson to be seen in a more positive light.]

__F__ 2. Experts automatically reject the claims of people who say they accomplished amazing feats. [This is a *faulty* inference, though experts carefully study any proof of such a claim.]

__C__ 3. People discuss and debate record-breaking events for many years after they happen. [This is a *correct* inference. Experts are still debating Peary and Henson's 1909 expedition.]

__F__ 4. It would have been safer for Avery to begin his expedition in January. [This is a *faulty* inference, since January in the Arctic is even colder than March.]

__C__ 5. Avery and his team probably lost weight on their trip. [This is a *correct* inference because they burned more calories each day than they took in.]

Score 5 points for each correct answer.

__25__ **Total Score:** Making Inferences

D Using Words Precisely

Each numbered sentence below contains an underlined word or phrase from the article. Following the sentence are three definitions. One definition is closest to the meaning of the underlined word. One definition is opposite or nearly opposite. Label those two definitions using the following key. Do not label the remaining definition.

C—Closest   **O—Opposite or Nearly Opposite**

1. These experts point out several underlined inconsistent entries in Peary's notes.
    __O__ a. in agreement
    __C__ b. conflicting
    ____ c. interesting

2. They also wonder how Peary's team overcame the seemingly insurmountable obstacle of crossing the frozen Arctic Ocean.
    __O__ a. easy to overcome
    ____ b. well known
    __C__ c. not able to be conquered

3. Avery and his team faced formidable challenges crossing the Arctic Ocean in a time of increased global warming.
    __C__ a. impressive and difficult
    ____ b. ancient
    __O__ c. easy to overcome

4. Beyond all this, the team supplemented everything with butter, butter, and more butter.
    ____ a. enjoyed
    __C__ b. added to, in order to make more complete
    __O__ c. took away from

5. Luckily, the combination of the dogs' weight and their <u>frenetic</u> swimming and groping did not pull the sled in behind them.

_C_ a. in a hurried and excited manner

_O_ b. easy going; calm

_____ c. frightened or worried

_15_ Score 3 points for each correct C answer.

_10_ Score 2 points for each correct O answer.

_25_ **Total Score**: Using Words Precisely

Enter the four total scores in the spaces below, and add them together to find your Reading Comprehension Score. Then record your score on the graph on page 57.

Score	Question Type	Sample Lesson
25	Finding the Main Idea	
25	Recalling Facts	
25	Making Inferences	
25	Using Words Precisely	
100	**Reading Comprehension Score**	

Author's Approach

Put an X in the box next to the correct answer.

1. What is the author's purpose in writing this article?
   - ☐ a. to encourage the reader to learn more about the Arctic
   - ☒ b. to inform the reader about an important expedition
   - ☐ c. to express an opinion about whether Peary and Henson really reached the North Pole

2. From the statements below, choose the one that you believe the author would agree with.
   - ☒ a. Avery did a good job of re-creating Peary's expedition.
   - ☐ b. The experts who doubt that Peary and Henson reached the North Pole are being ridiculous.
   - ☐ c. Avery and his team could have reached the pole more quickly if they had wanted to.

3. The author tells this story mainly by
   - ☒ a. describing events in the order they happened.
   - ☐ b. comparing different topics.
   - ☐ c. using his imagination or creativity.

4. Considering the statement from the article "Counting down the last 60 feet on the Global Positioning System, they walked side-by-side to the top of the world," you can conclude that the author wants the reader to think that
   - ☐ a. Avery was not feeling strong enough to walk alone.
   - ☐ b. Avery was too nervous to walk to the Pole alone.
   - ☒ c. the team members wanted to share the victory equally.

_4_ Number of correct answers

Record your personal assessment of your work on the Critical Thinking Chart on page 58.

CRITICAL THINKING

Summarizing and Paraphrasing

Put an X in the box next to the correct answer.

1. Choose the best one-sentence paraphrase for the following sentence from the article: "Finally, the pressure ridges—those towering walls of ice formed when one sheet of ice pushes into another—may be smaller in the 21st century, but they are more numerous and less stable."

☐ a. Today there are more pressure ridges, the tall walls of ice created when one ice sheet pushes against another. [This paraphrase leaves out important details.]

☒ b. Although in the 21st century the pressure ridges (towering ice walls that result from the pressure of one ice sheet on another) may be smaller, there are more of them and they are not as stable as before. [This sentence correctly rephrases the sentence.]

☐ c. Recently the pressure ridges (the huge walls of ice made when one sheet of ice pushes against another) have grown larger and have also become rarer and less stable. [This paraphrase contains errors.]

2. Below are summaries of the article. Choose the summary that says all the most important things about the article but in the fewest words.

☒ a. In 2005 Tom Avery and his crew re-created the 1909 polar expedition of Robert Peary and Matthew Henson, proving to critics that it was possible for Peary and his crew to have reached the North Pole on foot in 37 days. [This summary says all the most important things about the article in the fewest words.]

☐ b. Adventurer Tom Avery endured blizzards, freezing temperatures, and bad-tasting food to reach the North Pole in just under 37 days. [This summary leaves out important information.]

☐ c. Tom Avery wanted to prove that Robert Peary's feat was possible, so he made sure that his March 2005 expedition duplicated the teams, sleds, and route used by Peary in 1909. [This summary uses a great many words and still leaves out important information.]

> _2_ Number of correct answers
>
> Record your personal assessment of your work on the Critical Thinking Chart on page 58.

Record your personal assessment of your work on the Critical Thinking Chart on page 58.

Critical Thinking

Follow the directions provided for questions 1, 3, and 4. Put an X in the box next to the correct answer for question 2.

1. For each statement below, write O if it expresses an opinion or write F if it expresses a fact.

_O_ a. The journey to the North Pole was harder for Avery than it had been for Peary and Henson. [This statement is an _opinion;_ it cannot be proved.]

_F_ b. Avery completed the journey in 36 days, 22 hours, and 11 minutes. [This statement is a _fact;_ it can be proved.]

_F_ c. Avery's crew consumed about 7,000 calories per day. [This statement is a _fact;_ it can be proved.]

2. From what the article told about experts in the polar community, you can predict that after Avery's success

☐ a. the experts will be embarrassed that they ever doubted Peary and Henson's story.

☐ b. all the experts will agree that Peary and Henson were the first to reach the North Pole.

☒ c. some will still doubt that Peary and Henson reached the North Pole in 37 days.

3. Choose from the letters below to correctly complete the following statement. Write the letters on the lines.

The article states that _a_ and _c_ are different.

a. the total area of open water on the Arctic Ocean in 1909

b. the total area of open water on the Indian Ocean in 2005

c. the total area of open water on the Arctic Ocean in 2005

4. In which paragraph did you find your information or details to answer question 3?

paragraph 5

---

4 Number of correct answers

Record your personal assessment of your work on the Critical Thinking Chart on page 58.

Personal Response

What new question do you have about this topic?

[Write a question about something else you'd like to know

about Arctic expeditions or about the Arctic region in

general.]

Which concepts or ideas from the article were difficult to understand?

[Record any confusing ideas or concepts from the article here.]

Which were easy to understand?

[Record any concepts or ideas that you understood well.]

CRITICAL THINKING

Self-Assessment

To get the most out of the *Above & Beyond* series, you need to take charge of your own progress in improving your reading comprehension and critical thinking skills. Here are some of the features that help you work on those essential skills.

Reading Comprehension Exercises. Complete these exercises immediately after reading the article. They help you recall what you have read, understand the stated and implied main ideas, and add words to your working vocabulary.

Critical Thinking Skills Exercises. These exercises help you focus on the author's approach and purpose, recognize and generate summaries and paraphrases, and identify relationships between ideas.

Personal Response and Self-Assessment. Questions in this category help you relate the articles to your personal experience and give you the opportunity to evaluate your understanding of the information in that lesson.

Compare and Contrast Charts. At the end of each unit you will complete a Compare and Contrast chart. The completed chart helps you see what the articles have in common and gives you an opportunity to explore your own ideas about the topics discussed in the articles.

The Graphs. The graphs and charts at the end of each unit enable you to keep track of your progress. Check your graphs regularly with your teacher. Decide whether your progress is satisfactory or whether you need additional work on some skills. What types of exercises are you having difficulty with? Talk with your teacher about ways to work on the skills in which you need the most practice.

Seeing the World by Bicycle

Traveling by bicycle has allowed Dervla Murphy to visit remote places that most tourists never see.

Sometimes the simplest things can inspire a lifetime passion. That is what happened to young Dervla Murphy in 1941. On her tenth birthday, Murphy got two presents: her first bicycle and a world atlas. Putting the two together, she soon hatched a plan. Someday she would bike from her home in Ireland to a distant land, a place that at the time seemed exotic to her—India!

2　　When Murphy told people about her ambition, they just laughed. In those days the idea of a woman biking thousands of miles alone *was* laughable. No woman back then did that sort of thing. Today, of course, people's ideas about extreme sports and world adventures have changed. There are hundreds of biking tours through countries such as Vietnam, South Africa, Mongolia, and Morocco. Men and women are now encouraged to test themselves physically in many different ways. Today no one would laugh at a woman who said she was going to bungee-jump off a 125-foot bridge or climb Mount Everest or run a marathon in Death Valley. During Murphy's early life, however, most people thought any woman wanting to bike solo from Ireland to India was just a passionate dreamer.

3   Childhood fantasies like Murphy's have a tendency to burn out over time. New priorities push the old plans aside, and they slowly fade away. One of life's unexpected demands caught Murphy when she was just 14 years old. Her mother became disabled by rheumatoid arthritis, and so Murphy left school to take care of her. For the next 16 years, Murphy nursed her invalid mother. Mrs. Murphy, however, understood her daughter's desire to explore the world on a bike, and so each year she insisted that Murphy allow someone else to care for her for a few weeks. This freed Murphy to take a series of month-long biking trips to Spain, France, and Germany. Murphy paid for them by writing articles for Irish newspapers. When Murphy's mother passed away in 1962, Murphy turned her attention back to that deferred dream and started planning seriously for a solo bike trip to India.

4   From her previous bike trips, Murphy knew about some of the challenges she would face. The bicycle itself would have to be extremely rugged and fully capable of going up and down the mountains she would cross. She chose a no-nonsense 36-pound Armstrong Cadet she nicknamed "Roz." When fully loaded, the bike nearly doubled in weight. To avoid trouble with shifting gears, she removed the derailleur, the device that shifts gears. This made climbing hills harder, but her bike was less likely to break down. Murphy also shipped spare tires to certain cities along her planned route in case of emergency. Finally, aware that she could meet serious trouble, she learned to shoot a pistol, and she tucked that into her travel bag.

5   Murphy knew one thing for sure—she didn't want to bike in India in the heat of summer. Unfortunately, given that the trip would take six months, she could only avoid India's summer heat by leaving Ireland in the middle of Europe's winter. The winter of 1963 was one of the worst ever. Murphy tried to bike through it, but within days, she was battling snow and freezing temperatures. One day, in the mountains of France, the road disappeared in a blanket of snow. She had no choice but to take the train to Italy.

6   Even as she headed south, the brutal weather continued to plague her. In Yugoslavia, slippery black ice made bike riding too dangerous, so she accepted a lift from a passing truck driver. The driver struggled with the icy conditions until finally, in the middle of the night, he lost control and the truck slammed into a tree.

World traveler Dervla Murphy shaped a career out of her love of bicycling.

Murphy left her bike next to the injured driver and began walking to a nearby village to seek help. She hadn't gone far when an animal leaped out of the dark and attacked her. She felt its teeth sink into her shoulder while another creature growled and nipped at her ankles. She was not sure whether these were wolves or dogs crazed with hunger, but she understood that they meant to kill her. Murphy reacted quickly. She pulled out her gun and got off two shots, killing the animal at her neck and wounding the one at her feet. Then she ran as fast as she could until she reached the village, where police rescued her, her bike, and the truck driver.

7   Murphy needed her gun on one other occasion, too. In Iran, she was resting by the side of the road when three men, each carrying a spade, approached her. Murphy rose to greet them, but the men were not interested in friendship. Instead, two of them grabbed her bike and the third threatened her with his spade. Murphy quickly pulled out her gun and fired one shot in the air, then leveled her aim at the man closest to her. Luckily, that was all it took. The men dropped her bike and their spades and fled. Although this experience was unnerving, it was balanced out by the many kind and considerate people Murphy met. One day, for example, she was napping by the side of a road in Afghanistan when someone came by and put up a tent over her to shield her from the sun, doing it so quietly that Murphy didn't wake up.

8   As Murphy neared India, she faced one final challenge: the immense Babusar Pass in Pakistan. Although temperatures reached 120 degrees in the valley below, the path was high and covered by a glacier. Snow swirled wildly in the bitter wind. As Murphy hauled herself and her bike along the frozen pass, the trail was so slippery that sometimes she had to crawl on all fours with her bike on her shoulders. She reached the top just before sunset. Her strength waning, Murphy knew she had to go back down very quickly or risk freezing to death. Luckily, she spotted a caravan traveling about a mile below her. Biking down the winding trail would take too long, so she gathered her courage and began sliding down the side of the glacier. The astonished men of the caravan cheered when she landed safely at the bottom. The final 120 miles to Rawalpindi in India was an easy ride, which seemed almost like a reward for her troubles.

9   At the end of this triumphant trip, Dervla Murphy wrote a book about her adventures called *Full Tilt: Ireland to India with a Bicycle*. And she didn't stop there. She continued to challenge herself, biking to countries all over the world, including Madagascar, Kenya, Russia, and Peru. In 2008, at the age of 77, Murphy journeyed to Cuba. By then, she had written nearly two dozen travel adventure books. In all her travels, biking remained her preferred mode of transportation. As she told one reporter in 2010, "You never want your traveling to be too easy." ✳

If you have been timed while reading this article, enter your reading time below. Then turn to the Words-per-Minute Table on page 55 and look up your reading speed (words per minute). Enter your reading speed on the graph on page 56.

Reading Time: Lesson 1

_____ : _____
  Minutes   *Seconds*

A Finding the Main Idea

One statement below expresses the main idea of the article. One statement is too general, or too broad. The other statement explains only part of the article; it is too narrow. Label the statements using the following key:

M—Main Idea   **B—Too Broad**   **N—Too Narrow**

_____ 1. Dervla Murphy faced many challenges as she fulfilled her childhood dream of riding a bike solo from Ireland to India.

_____ 2. After receiving a bike for her tenth birthday, Dervla Murphy dreamed of riding from Ireland to India.

_____ 3. Dervla Murphy is one of the many adventurous people who travel all over the world by bicycle.

_____ Score 15 points for a correct M answer.

_____ Score 5 points for each correct B or N answer.

_____ **Total Score**: Finding the Main Idea

B Recalling Facts

How well do you remember the facts in the article? Put an X in the box next to the answer that correctly completes each statement about the article.

1. Dervla Murphy received her first bike in
   ☐ a. 1962.
   ☐ b. 1941.
   ☐ c. 1950.

2. Dervla Murphy thought her trip to India would take
   ☐ a. a year.
   ☐ b. nine months.
   ☐ c. six months.

3. Murphy was attacked by wild animals in
   ☐ a. Yugoslavia.
   ☐ b. Pakistan.
   ☐ c. India.

4. When Murphy was threatened by three men in Iran, she
   ☐ a. shot two of them.
   ☐ b. fired one shot in the air and scared the men away.
   ☐ c. ran as fast as she could to a nearby village.

5. At the age of 77, Dervla Murphy traveled to
   ☐ a. Kenya.
   ☐ b. Madagascar.
   ☐ c. Cuba.

Score 5 points for each correct answer.

_____ **Total Score**: Recalling Facts

C Making Inferences

When you combine your own experiences and information from a text to draw a conclusion that is not directly stated in that text, you are making an inference. Below are five statements that may or may not be inferences based on information in the article. Label the statements using the following key:

C—Correct Inference   **F—Faulty Inference**

_____ 1. Murphy could write interesting stories.

_____ 2. Murphy was a very strong, athletic woman.

_____ 3. Murphy would not have biked to India if she had known how difficult it would be.

_____ 4. Murphy resented having to take care of her mother.

_____ 5. In 1963, people in India, Iran, and Pakistan were not used to seeing women riding bikes.

> Score 5 points for each correct answer.
>
> _____ **Total Score**: Making Inferences

D Using Words Precisely

Each numbered sentence below contains an underlined word or phrase from the article. Following the sentence are three definitions. One definition is closest to the meaning of the underlined word. One definition is opposite or nearly opposite. Label those two definitions using the following key. Do not label the remaining definition.

C—Closest   **O—Opposite or Nearly Opposite**

1. Someday she would bike from her home in Ireland to a distant land, a place that at the time seemed <u>exotic</u> to her—India!

   _____ a. ordinary

   _____ b. excitingly unfamiliar

   _____ c. faraway

2. For the next 16 years, Murphy nursed her <u>invalid</u> mother.

   _____ a. unhappy

   _____ b. healthy

   _____ c. sickly

3. When Murphy's mother passed away, Murphy turned her attention back to that <u>deferred</u> dream.

   _____ a. delayed

   _____ b. hurried

   _____ c. favorite

4. Although Murphy's experience with the three men in Iran was <u>unnerving</u>, it was balanced out by the kind people Murphy met.

   _____ a. daring

   _____ b. upsetting

   _____ c. soothing

5. Her strength <u>waning</u>, Murphy knew she had to go down the glacier quickly or risk freezing to death.

_____ a. fading away

_____ b. encouraging

_____ c. increasing

_____ Score 3 points for each correct C answer.

_____ Score 2 points for each correct O answer.

_____ **Total Score:** Using Words Precisely

Enter the four total scores in the spaces below, and add them together to find your Reading Comprehension Score. Then record your score on the graph on page 57.

Score	Question Type	Lesson 1
_____	Finding the Main Idea	
_____	Recalling Facts	
_____	Making Inferences	
_____	Using Words Precisely	
_____	**Reading Comprehension Score**	

Author's Approach

Put an X in the box next to the correct answer.

1. The author uses the first sentence of the article to
   - ☐ a. inform the reader about Dervla Murphy's dream.
   - ☐ b. stimulate the reader's interest and curiosity.
   - ☐ c. soothe the reader.

2. The author tells this story mainly by
   - ☐ a. recounting Murphy's experiences on her trip to India.
   - ☐ b. explaining in detail the route that Murphy took on her trip to India.
   - ☐ c. describing the weather and geography of the countries Murphy traveled through on her way to India.

3. Judging by statements from the article, you can conclude that the author wants the reader to think that
   - ☐ a. Murphy made a lot of mistakes.
   - ☐ b. Murphy took a lot of foolish chances.
   - ☐ c. Murphy is a remarkable woman.

4. In this article, "Childhood fantasies like Murphy's have a tendency to burn out over time" means
   - ☐ a. in recent years, people have stopped having fantasies like Murphy's.
   - ☐ b. people rarely fulfill their childhood dreams.
   - ☐ c. people never fulfill their childhood dreams.

_____ Number of correct answers

Record your personal assessment of your work on the Critical Thinking Chart on page 58.

CRITICAL THINKING

Summarizing and Paraphrasing

Follow the directions provided for questions 1 and 3. Put an X in the box next to the correct answer for question 2.

1. Complete the following one-sentence summary of the article using the lettered phrases from the phrase bank below. Write the letters on the lines.

Phrase Bank:
  a. a summary of Dervla Murphy's life since 1963
  b. her trip to India
  c. her planning for the trip to India

The article "Seeing the World by Bicycle" begins with _____, goes on to describe _____, and ends with _____.

2. Choose the sentence that correctly restates the following sentence from the article: "Even as she headed south, the brutal weather continued to plague her."

☐ a. Despite Dervla's traveling south, the horrible weather kept causing problems.

☐ b. Although Dervla turned south, the terrible weather still made her sick.

☐ c. When she turned south, she ran into bad weather.

3. Reread the last paragraph of the article. Below, write a summary of the paragraph in no more than 25 words.

_____
_____
_____
_____

Reread your summary and decide whether it covers the important ideas in the paragraph. Next, decide how to shorten the summary to 15 words or less without leaving out any essential information. Write the summary below.

_____
_____
_____

_____ Number of correct answers

Record your personal assessment of your work on the Critical Thinking Chart on page 58.

Critical Thinking

Follow the directions provided for questions 1, 3 and 4. Put an X in the box next to the correct answer for the other questions.

1. For each statement below, write O if it expresses an opinion or write F if it expresses a fact.

_____ a. Dervla Murphy wrote a book about her adventures.

_____ b. Crossing the Babusar Pass was the most difficult part of Murphy's trip to India.

_____ c. From the time she was 10 years old, Murphy had a dream of biking from Ireland to India.

2. Using the information in the second paragraph, you can predict that

☐ a. women will lose interest in extreme sports.

☐ b. there will be no new adventures.

☐ c. women will continue to challenge themselves athletically.

CRITICAL THINKING

3. Choose from the letters below to correctly complete the following statement. Write the letters on the lines.

On the positive side, _____, but on the negative side _____.

   a. Murphy didn't want to take care of her mother

   b. Murphy met many kind people

   c. three men tried to rob Murphy

4. Choose from the letters below to correctly complete the following statement. Write the letters on the lines.

According to the article, _____ caused _____ , and the effect

was that _____ .

   a. the truck driver to lose control of his truck

   b. the truck slammed into a tree

   c. the icy road conditions in Yugoslavia

5. From what the article told about Dervla Murphy, you can conclude that she

   ☐ a. is a brave woman.

   ☐ b. does not plan her trips well.

   ☐ c. never returned to India.

_____ Number of correct answers

Record your personal assessment of your work on the Critical Thinking Chart on page 58.

Personal Response

A question I would like answered by Dervla Murphy is

_____

_____

_____

_____

Self-Assessment

The part I found most difficult about the article was

_____

_____

_____

_____

I found this difficult because

_____

_____

_____

_____

_____

CRITICAL THINKING

Lost and Found

The free-flowing Tuichi River in Bolivia changes from calm waters to powerful rapids and waterfalls.

After two years of routine service in the Israeli navy, 22-year-old Yossi Ghinsberg was ready for a big adventure. He sought wild journeys and exotic destinations. "I wanted to be like the heroes of the books I read," he said. "I was obsessed with the idea of exploration." To satisfy his desire, Ghinsberg traveled to South America in 1981 and began backpacking from place to place. Eventually he met two fellow travelers, an American named Kevin Wallace and a Swiss man named Marcus. As these three meandered through the streets of La Paz, Bolivia, they imagined great adventures for themselves. Then one day they met Karl, and nothing was ever the same again.

2   Karl told the young men that he was an Austrian geologist with extensive knowledge of the Bolivian jungle. In fact, he said, for the right price he would be willing to lead them on an expedition to a remote village unknown to the rest of the world. Not only was this village untouched by modern society, but it contained a gold mine brimming with riches. To an objective listener, Karl's story might have sounded too good to be true, but Ghinsberg swallowed the story without hesitation. "I wanted it so badly that I literally begged him to take me with him on this adventure," Ghinsberg recalled. A few days after meeting him, Ghinsberg, Wallace, and Marcus flew with Karl to an airstrip in the northwest corner of Bolivia. From there, they hiked four days to one last tiny outpost and then headed off into the Amazon rain forest.

3   The journey was difficult from the beginning. "The environment was harsh," Ghinsberg later recalled. "There were tensions, the food was basic—we shot and ate monkeys, among other things." As they pushed farther and farther into the Amazon jungle, fatigue set in. Beyond that, there was a growing disenchantment with Karl. At first, there were little things. For instance, the group had purchased 10 lighters for making fires, but Karl traded nine of them away at the last outpost, leaving them without a backup in case of an emergency. In time the questions about Karl became more serious. How much jungle experience did he really have, and why was he having so much trouble locating the village? Making matters worse, Marcus developed trench foot, a condition brought on by the damp jungle conditions. Trench foot brings pain, swelling, and an awful stench as the flesh of the feet literally rots away.

4   After 10 days of misery, Ghinsberg, Wallace, and Marcus halted the expedition. Karl agreed to take them back, but when they returned to the outpost, they still faced four days of hard hiking to reach the airstrip. Hoping to avoid this, the men built a raft and attempted to float down the Tuichi River to the airstrip. Unfortunately, the river proved as treacherous as the jungle, and they quickly became unnerved by its swift current and increasingly strong rapids. Making matters worse, Karl announced that he couldn't swim. Wallace urged them to continue on the raft anyway, but Karl refused and, after a heated discussion, the group split up. Wallace and Ghinsberg remained on the raft, while the other two set out on foot.

5   The fate of Karl and Marcus remains a mystery to this day; neither man was ever seen again. As for Ghinsberg and Wallace, they soon found themselves headed for a series of steep waterfalls. Wallace scrambled to the shore at the last minute, but Ghinsberg

A jaguar's camouflage coat helps it blend with the jungle's shifting shadows and light.

didn't act quickly enough. The raft hit a rock and was smashed to pieces, and Ghinsberg was swept over a falls. For 15 minutes he tumbled down one falls, then another, and then another. Then the current carried him through a canyon, and he finally washed up on a narrow riverbank. Ghinsberg realized he was completely alone. He had no way to make a fire, no equipment, no weapon, no raft, and no Wallace—he had nothing but what he could make or find on his own.

6   Ghinsberg's ordeal had just begun. For the next 19 days he tried to follow the river as it wound through the thick, menacing jungle. Thousands of insects swarmed him, and their bites caused Ghinsberg to develop a dangerous blood infection. A fungus began to grow on his feet that turned the skin red and rotten. He decided to walk in the water to cool his feet, but the river was infested with leeches that attached to his skin and sucked his blood. When he rested on the shore, bugs crawled over him and stung him severely. Twice he sank chest-deep into quicksand, and one night as he lay curled up on the jungle floor a jaguar crept up to him and sniffed his face.

7   As the days passed, Ghinsberg grew progressively weaker. Through it all, he urged himself to find food and to carry on. Ghinsberg couldn't reach any high-growing fruit, so he scavenged rotting pieces that

had fallen to the ground. He also searched for birds' nests so he could eat the eggs. He was terribly lonely, weak, and injured, but he kept panic away by repeating to himself, "You're a man of action. Don't cry. Don't break down."

8   Torrential rainstorms moved in and flooded the river, sweeping away all remnants of food. Ghinsberg staggered on, but by then, as he later said, "I was just skin and bones." His feet were so sore he could barely walk. "I shook a tree full of fire ants on my head just to have some pain to distract me from my aching feet so that I could continue to walk." At last, his feet became so inflamed he was reduced to crawling.

9   After 19 days in the jungle, Ghinsberg literally could not travel any more. He collapsed, barely conscious, on the riverbank. After some time, he heard a buzzing sound and assumed it was more swarms of insects that had come to feast on him. When the buzz grew louder than insects, he looked up—and saw Wallace coming toward him in a boat! Ghinsberg thought he was hallucinating, but the image was real. Wallace had made his way to safety and had hired local villagers to guide him up the river to look for his friend. Wallace later said they would have stopped the search before reaching Ghinsberg, but they could not find a place to turn around.

So they sailed farther upstream to land the boat, and the place where they stopped was exactly where Ghinsberg had collapsed on the beach. Wallace and the guides helped the emaciated Ghinsberg into the boat, and they celebrated in a joyful reunion.

10   Ghinsberg later learned that Karl had made up the story about the gold and the village, and he had fooled other tourists, too. "I don't think he was a bad guy," Ghinsberg later said of Karl. "He wanted to take us into this harsh environment to see if we could deal with it." Yossi Ghinsberg ultimately made a full recovery, but the ordeal changed his life, he said. "That feeling of touching death has never left me." ✷

If you have been timed while reading this article, enter your reading time below. Then turn to the Words-per-Minute Table on page 55 and look up your reading speed (words per minute). Enter your reading speed on the graph on page 56.

Reading Time: Lesson 2

_____ : _____
   Minutes   Seconds

A Finding the Main Idea

One statement below expresses the main idea of the article. One statement is too general, or too broad. The other statement explains only part of the article; it is too narrow. Label the statements using the following key:

M—Main Idea   **B—Too Broad**   **N—Too Narrow**

_____   1.   Yossi Ghinsberg listened to a fellow traveler who told him about a village deep in the Amazon jungle.

_____   2.   Yossi Ghinsberg's adventure involved many problems.

_____   3.   The journey for Yossi Ghinsberg and three other travelers into the Amazon jungle turned into a struggle for survival.

_____   Score 15 points for a correct M answer.

_____   Score 5 points for each correct B or N answer.

_____   **Total Score**: Finding the Main Idea

B Recalling Facts

How well do you remember the facts in the article? Put an X in the box next to the answer that correctly completes each statement about the article.

1.   Karl told Ghinsberg and his friends that he was from
  ☐ a.   Austria.
  ☐ b.   Switzerland.
  ☐ c.   America.

2.   Marcus suffered from
  ☐ a.   a dangerous blood infection.
  ☐ b.   blood-sucking leeches.
  ☐ c.   trench foot.

3.   After the group of travelers broke up, Ghinsberg remained on the raft with
  ☐ a.   Marcus.
  ☐ b.   Wallace.
  ☐ c.   Karl.

4.   When Ghinsberg was alone, he ate
  ☐ a.   monkeys.
  ☐ b.   rotten fruit.
  ☐ c.   leeches.

5.   Ghinsberg traveled alone for
  ☐ a.   4 days.
  ☐ b.   10 days.
  ☐ c.   19 days.

Score 5 points for each correct answer.

_____   **Total Score**: Recalling Facts

C Making Inferences

When you combine your own experiences and information from a text to draw a conclusion that is not directly stated in that text, you are making an inference. Below are five statements that may or may not be inferences based on information in the article. Label the statements using the following key:

C—Correct Inference   **F—Faulty Inference**

_____ 1. Ghinsberg was a very trusting young man.

_____ 2. Karl was a man who could easily persuade others.

_____ 3. No person could live for very long in the Bolivian rain forest.

_____ 4. None of the four travelers had any knowledge of the Bolivian jungle.

_____ 5. Ghinsberg did not climb trees to get fruit because he was weak and his feet hurt.

Score 5 points for each correct answer.

_____ **Total Score:** Making Inferences

D Using Words Precisely

Each numbered sentence below contains an underlined word or phrase from the article. Following the sentence are three definitions. One definition is closest to the meaning of the underlined word. One definition is opposite or nearly opposite. Label those two definitions using the following key. Do not label the remaining definition.

C—Closest   **O—Opposite or Nearly Opposite**

1. The three travelers <u>meandered</u> through the streets of La Paz, Bolivia.

_____ a. went directly toward a goal

_____ b. wandered without any fixed destination

_____ c. looked for something

2. Karl told the young men that he was an Austrian geologist with <u>extensive</u> knowledge of the Bolivian jungle.

_____ a. very thorough, detailed

_____ b. worthless

_____ c. limited

3. As they hiked through the jungle, there was a growing <u>disenchantment</u> with Karl.

_____ a. satisfaction

_____ b. displeasure

_____ c. discussion

4. Ghinsberg tried to follow the river through the thick, <u>menacing</u> jungle.

_____ a. uncontrolled

_____ b. friendly

_____ c. dangerous

5. The guides helped the <u>emaciated</u> Ghinsberg into the boat.

_____ a. exhausted

_____ b. overweight

_____ c. extremely thin

_____ Score 3 points for each correct C answer.

_____ Score 2 points for each correct O answer.

_____ **Total Score**: Using Words Precisely

Enter the four total scores in the spaces below, and add them together to find your Reading Comprehension Score. Then record your score on the graph on page 57.

Score	Question Type	Lesson 2
_____	Finding the Main Idea	
_____	Recalling Facts	
_____	Making Inferences	
_____	Using Words Precisely	
_____	**Reading Comprehension Score**	

Author's Approach

Put an X in the box next to the correct answer.

1. The main purpose of the first paragraph is to

☐ a. introduce the four travelers to the reader.

☐ b. inform the reader about Ghinsberg's life in Israel.

☐ c. explain how Ghinsberg met the other three travelers.

2. What is the author's purpose in writing this article?

☐ a. to warn the reader about the dangers of traveling in the Bolivian jungle

☐ b. to relate an amazing story of survival

☐ c. to describe what happens when you listen to strangers

3. The author tells this story mainly by

☐ a. describing the dangers the travelers found in the Amazon jungle.

☐ b. comparing the experiences of the four travelers.

☐ c. describing events of Ghinsberg's journey in the order they happened.

4. Considering the statement from the article "At last, his feet became so inflamed he was reduced to crawling," you can conclude that the author wants the reader to think that

☐ a. Ghinsberg was so determined to survive that he did not let pain stop him.

☐ b. Ghinsberg looked for the easy way to do things.

☐ c. Ghinsberg had to suffer the consequences of not taking care of himself.

_____ Number of correct answers

Record your personal assessment of your work on the Critical Thinking Chart on page 58.

Summarizing and Paraphrasing

Put an X in the box next to the correct answer for question 1. Follow the directions provided for question 2.

1. Choose the best one-sentence paraphrase for the following sentence from the article: "After 10 days of misery, Ghinsberg, Wallace, and Marcus halted the expedition."

   ☐ a. After only 10 days, Ghinsberg, Wallace, and Marcus started to feel miserable.

   ☐ b. Ghinsberg, Wallace, and Marcus stopped feeling miserable after 10 days of hiking.

   ☐ c. The three travelers brought the journey to an end after suffering for 10 days.

2. Reread paragraph 9 in the article. Below, write a summary of the paragraph in no more than 25 words.

   _____

   _____

   _____

   _____

   Reread your summary and decide whether it covers the important ideas in the paragraph. Next, decide how to shorten the summary to 15 words or less without leaving out any essential information. Write this summary below.

   _____

   _____

   _____ Number of correct answers

   Record your personal assessment of your work on the Critical Thinking Chart on page 58.

Critical Thinking

Follow the directions provided for questions 1 and 2. Put an X next to the correct answer for the other questions.

1. For each statement below, write O if it expresses an opinion or write F if it expresses a fact.

   _____ a. Karl was an evil man.

   _____ b. The city of La Paz is in Bolivia.

   _____ c. The Amazon jungle is the most dangerous place in the world.

2. Using what you know about Yossi Ghinsberg and what is told about Kevin Wallace in the article, name three ways Ghinsberg is similar to Wallace and three ways Ghinsberg is different from Wallace. Cite the paragraph number(s) where you found details in the article to support your conclusion.

   Similarities

   _____

   _____

   _____

   Differences

   _____

   _____

   _____

3. What was the effect of the thousands of bug bites that Ghinsberg received when he was traveling alone through the jungle?

   ☐ a. painfully sore feet

   ☐ b. a dangerous blood infection

   ☐ c. trench foot

4. Of the following theme categories, which would this story fit into?

☐ a. Plants and Animals of the Jungle

☐ b. Tall Tales

☐ c. Amazing Stories

5. Judging by events in the article, you can conclude that

☐ a. all rivers have rapids and waterfalls.

☐ b. traveling in a jungle is never safe.

☐ c. it is wise to check on a story that sounds too good to be true.

_____ Number of correct answers

Record your personal assessment of your work on the Critical Thinking Chart on page 58.

Personal Response

What do you think was Yossi Ghinsberg's biggest mistake?

_____

_____

_____

_____

Self-Assessment

I'm proud of how I answered question #_____ in section _____ because

_____

_____

_____

_____

_____

_____

_____

_____

Sailing Solo

Hilary Lister is shown on the far right with her support team during trials for her record-breaking sailing attempt.

In 2003 all the doors of life seemed to be closed to 31-year-old Hilary Lister. Opportunity was unknown to Lister, a quadriplegic, paralyzed from the neck down by a rare degenerative condition known as reflex sympathetic dystrophy. Although Lister couldn't move her limbs, she could still feel pain—and the pain was relentless. The only way she could diminish it was with a steady dose of painkillers. As she put it, "The pain is in my hips, my knees, my ankles, my shoulders, my wrists, pretty much everywhere." Knowing that she would never recover the use of her legs, arms, or hands, Lister became depressed and withdrawn. She spent endless hours staring out the window of her home in southeast England.

2 One day Lister received an unexpected invitation from a friend who offered to take her to a lake for a special day-long sailing program for severely disabled people. "I said yes immediately, basically because I hadn't been out of the house in three months," she recalled. "As soon as they put me in a boat, it was like having another dimension." Out on the water, she experienced the sensation of freedom and pure joy she hadn't known for years. It did not eliminate her pain, but it helped distract her from it. "Within 30 seconds, I'd fallen in love. I knew that I had to make sailing part of the rest of my life." Lister's mind clicked into gear. She began to wonder and then imagine that maybe, just maybe, she could learn to sail a boat by herself.

3 Hilary Lister had not always been a quadriplegic. As a young girl growing up in England, she had been active in many sports, including swimming, rugby, and hockey. She was fiercely independent, and she admits that she also was extremely competitive. When she was 11 years old, however, she began to develop pain in her knees. Her doctor dismissed the problem as "growing pains." By the time she was 15, the problem had grown so severe that she could no longer walk, and she found herself confined to a wheelchair. Doctors finally determined what was wrong when Lister was 17 years old, but by then the disease had progressed too far to be treated effectively. Little by little, her physical abilities slipped away until, by age 27, she couldn't move any part of her body below her neck.

4 After she had sailed, her competitive drive kicked in once again. Lister decided she wanted to sail solo across the English Channel. First she needed a boat specially equipped just for her—and then she had to

Lister sails her 20-foot puff boat "Me Too."

learn to sail it. A friend named Matt Debicki rigged a sailboat that could be sailed by sipping and puffing on two plastic tubes. Each tube was connected to electric motors from old wheelchairs. One of the tubes moved the tiller, which controlled direction. A sip on this tube would turn the boat to the left; puffing into it would turn the boat to the right. The other tube controlled how fast the boat went. A sip into that tube would close down the sails, thereby reducing the boat's speed. A puff would open up the sails to catch more wind and increase the speed.

5   Although Lister soon learned how to maneuver the boat, she did need help with many aspects of sailing. Other people had to lower her into her specially designed chair and strap her in to keep her from falling forward in the choppy seas. The sip-puff mechanism then had to be lowered over her head so she could reach the tubes with her mouth. If it was a bright day, someone also needed to place a baseball cap on her head for sun protection. Whenever Lister went for a sail, a support crew followed her in a separate boat.

6   By 2005 Lister was ready to take on the English Channel. She departed from the town of Dover on the east coast of England in her 27-foot boat with her support team following close behind. By sipping and puffing, Lister steered and controlled the speed of her boat as it headed out into the English Channel. Six hours later an exhausted but exuberant Lister arrived in

Calais, France, 21 miles from where she had started. At that time, Lister's trip was the longest solo voyage ever by a quadriplegic.

7   Next, Lister became captivated by a much more difficult voyage. She wanted to sail around the coast of Britain, a trip of more than 1,500 miles. In June 2008 she set sail from Dover, but had to abandon the effort after 500 miles due to bad weather. The following year she tried again, but just before her departure, she was rushed to the hospital with breathing difficulties. Many thought this misfortune would mark the end of her dream. Yet after a couple of hours under observation, Lister left the hospital and returned to the harbor, insisting that she was ready to go.

8   For the next three months, Lister sailed around the coast of Britain in 40 separate day-long treks, with occasional days of rest. Whenever the weather turned bad, she was in danger of hypothermia because she couldn't reach down and pull a blanket over herself. Similarly, whenever the temperature rose, Lister was susceptible to overheating, since she couldn't unzip her jacket or roll up her sleeves. Luckily, her crew was never more than a radio call away. Besides the dangers she faced while sailing, there was the question of whether Lister's body would hold up long enough for her to finish. Often, when back on land for meals, she choked on food. Someone would have to turn her over and slap her on the back to dislodge the food. Sometimes she had trouble breathing and ended up

passing out. "My diaphragm isn't particularly efficient," Lister said. Everybody on the team provided her with mouth-to-mouth resuscitation at one time or another. "They give me five or six breaths, which is enough to pump me up and get me going."

9   Despite the setbacks and dangers, Hilary Lister persevered. On August 31, 2009, she completed her journey, arriving triumphantly back in Dover. Supporters lined the harbor to cheer her arrival. Paul Taroni, Lister's spokesperson, summed up what many people were thinking when he said, "This is an amazing triumph over adversity. Everything that went against her, Hilary overcame to do something truly inspirational. We are all so proud of her." ✳

If you have been timed while reading this article, enter your reading time below. Then turn to the Words-per-Minute Table on page 55 and look up your reading speed (words per minute). Enter your reading speed on the graph on page 56.

Reading Time: Lesson 3

_____ : _____
 Minutes   Seconds

A Finding the Main Idea

One statement below expresses the main idea of the article. One statement is too general, or too broad. The other statement explains only part of the article; it is too narrow. Label the statements using the following key:

M—Main Idea   **B—Too Broad**   **N—Too Narrow**

_____ 1. Despite being a quadriplegic, Hilary Lister managed to sail solo in a boat that was specially equipped for her.

_____ 2. Hilary Lister sailed a boat by sipping and puffing on two plastic tubes.

_____ 3. Because she is a quadriplegic, Hilary Lister has faced many challenges.

_____ Score 15 points for a correct M answer.

_____ Score 5 points for each correct B or N answer.

_____ **Total Score**: Finding the Main Idea

B Recalling Facts

How well do you remember the facts in the article? Put an X in the box next to the answer that correctly completes each statement about the article.

1. Lister is paralyzed from the neck down because of a
   - ☐ a. terrible accident.
   - ☐ b. rare disease.
   - ☐ c. condition present at her birth.

2. Lister began to develop pain in her knees at age
   - ☐ a. 11.
   - ☐ b. 15.
   - ☐ c. 17.

3. When the sails on a sailboat are closed down, the boat
   - ☐ a. will go faster.
   - ☐ b. will turn.
   - ☐ c. will slow down.

4. Lister's crossing of the English Channel was completed in
   - ☐ a. three months.
   - ☐ b. six hours.
   - ☐ c. two days.

5. The distance that Lister covered in her voyage around the coast of Britain was
   - ☐ a. 21 miles.
   - ☐ b. 500 miles.
   - ☐ c. more than 1,500 miles.

Score 5 points for each correct answer.

_____ **Total Score**: Recalling Facts

C Making Inferences

When you combine your own experiences and information from a text to draw a conclusion that is not directly stated in that text, you are making an inference. Below are five statements that may or may not be inferences based on information in the article. Label the statements using the following key:

C—Correct Inference   **F—Faulty Inference**

_____ 1. It is not unusual for people who have reflex sympathetic dystrophy, the disease that Lister suffers from, to become depressed.

_____ 2. Lister's doctors should have been able to diagnose her condition immediately.

_____ 3. Lister has friends who are generous and thoughtful.

_____ 4. There are many quadriplegics around the world who can sail solo.

_____ 5. Sailboats are easy to control.

Score 5 points for each correct answer.

_____ **Total Score**: Making Inferences

D Using Words Precisely

Each numbered sentence below contains an underlined word or phrase from the article. Following the sentence are three definitions. One definition is closest to the meaning of the underlined word. One definition is opposite or nearly opposite. Label those two definitions using the following key. Do not label the remaining definition.

C—Closest   **O—Opposite or Nearly Opposite**

1. Hilary Lister suffers from a rare <u>degenerative</u> condition.

_____ a. improving

_____ b. getting steadily worse

_____ c. inherited

2. An exhausted but <u>exuberant</u> Lister arrived in Calais, France.

_____ a. full of joy

_____ b. wide awake

_____ c. depressed

3. Lister became <u>captivated</u> by a much more difficult voyage.

_____ a. changed

_____ b. disgusted

_____ c. attracted

4. Despite the setbacks and dangers, Hilary Lister <u>persevered</u>.

_____ a. kept going

_____ b. gave up

_____ c. worried

5. "This is an amazing triumph over <u>adversity</u>."

_____ a. good luck

_____ b. sickness

_____ c. hard times

_____ Score 3 points for each correct C answer.

_____ Score 2 points for each correct O answer.

_____ **Total Score**: Using Words Precisely

Enter the four total scores in the spaces below, and add them together to find your Reading Comprehension Score. Then record your score on the graph on page 57.

Score	Question Type	Lesson 3
_____	Finding the Main Idea	
_____	Recalling Facts	
_____	Making Inferences	
_____	Using Words Precisely	
_____	**Reading Comprehension Score**	

Author's Approach

Put an X in the box next to the correct answer.

1. From the statements below, choose the one that you believe the author would agree with.

☐ a. All quadriplegics should learn how to sail.

☐ b. Lister never lost her competitive spirit.

☐ c. Lister has been lucky so far, but sailing solo is too dangerous for her to continue.

2. Considering the statement from the article, "Yet after a couple of hours under observation, Lister left the hospital and returned to the harbor, insisting that she was ready to go," you can conclude that the author wants the reader to think that

☐ a. Lister is a very determined person who is not easily prevented from achieving a goal.

☐ b. there really was no good reason for Lister to be in the hospital.

☐ c. Lister is in the hospital so often that she is always eager to get out and get back to sailing.

3. Which of the following statements from the article best describes Hilary Lister's achievements?

☐ a. "Out on the water, she experienced the sensation of freedom and pure joy she hadn't known for years."

☐ b. "She began to wonder and then imagine that maybe, just maybe, she could learn to sail a boat by herself."

☐ c. "Everything that went against her, Hilary overcame to do something truly inspirational."

_____ Number of correct answers

Record your personal assessment of your work on the Critical Thinking Chart on page 58.

Summarizing and Paraphrasing

Put an X in the box next to the correct answer.

1. Choose the best one-sentence paraphrase for the following sentence from the article: "Supporters lined the harbor to cheer her arrival."

   ☐ a. Well-wishers gathered at the port and applauded her when she arrived.

   ☐ b. Her fans were waiting for her arrival at the harbor.

   ☐ c. People were happy when she reached the harbor.

2. Read the statement about the article below. Then read the paraphrase of that statement. Choose the reason that best tells why the paraphrase does not say the same thing as the statement.

   Statement: Lister was fiercely independent, and she admits that she also was extremely competitive.

   Paraphrase: Lister greatly preferred to do things on her own.

   ☐ a. Paraphrase says too much.

   ☐ b. Paraphrase doesn't say enough.

   ☐ c. Paraphrase doesn't agree with the statement.

3. Below are summaries of the article. Choose the summary that says all the most important things about the article but in the fewest words.

   ☐ a. Hilary Lister has sailed solo across the English Channel and around the coast of Britain. Her many friends admire her competitive spirit.

   ☐ b. Hilary Lister is a quadriplegic who has inspired others by her achievements in sailing.

   ☐ c. Hilary Lister is a quadriplegic who sails on her own with the support of friends. She has sailed solo across the English Channel and around the coast of Britain.

_____ Number of correct answers

Record your personal assessment of your work on the Critical Thinking Chart on page 58.

Critical Thinking

Follow the directions provided for questions 1, 3, and 5. Put an X in the box next to the correct answer for the other questions.

1. For each statement below, write O if it expresses an opinion or write F if it expresses a fact.

   _____ a. Hilary Lister should not have risked her life to sail.

   _____ b. Reflex sympathetic dystrophy is a rare condition.

   _____ c. The town of Dover is on the east coast of England.

2. From the article, you can predict that, if her body is strong enough, Lister will

   ☐ a. design boats for other disabled people.

   ☐ b. quit sailing because she has achieved the goals she set for herself.

   ☐ c. continue sailing.

3. Reread paragraph 3. Then choose from the letters below to correctly complete the following statement. Write the letters on the lines.

   According to paragraph 3, _____ because _____.

   a. her disease had progressed too long without effective treatment

   b. her doctors finally diagnosed her condition

   c. Lister became a quadriplegic

4. From what the article told about Hilary Lister's friends and support crew, you can conclude that they

   ☐ a. took up sailing at the same time as Lister.

   ☐ b. are loyal and dependable.

   ☐ c. are medical experts.

5. Which paragraph provides evidence that supports your answer to question 4?

_____

_____ Number of correct answers

Record your personal assessment of your work on the Critical Thinking Chart on page 58.

Personal Response

How do you think Hilary Lister felt when she was first confined to a wheelchair?

_____

_____

_____

_____

_____

_____

Self-Assessment

The part I found most difficult about the article was

_____

_____

_____

_____

I found this part difficult because

_____

_____

_____

_____

_____

_____

_____

_____

_____

James Beckwourth

Man and Myth

S uppose you wanted to learn all you could about the American West in the early 19th century through the eyes of just one person. Choosing the life of explorer Jim Beckwourth would be a good way to do it. At one time or another, Beckwourth did just about everything a man in the pioneer days could do. Beckwourth would get bored with one adventure and then move on to the next. Over the course of his life, he was a beaver trapper, trading post owner, wilderness explorer, and a gold prospector. He also found excitement as a horse thief and a pioneer guide. Beckwourth also had extensive contact with Native American peoples. Sometimes he fought on their side, and sometimes he fought against them. He even became a war chief for the Crow.

2   Although there were other African Americans who lived fascinating lives in the Wild West too, only Beckwourth was featured in a book written during his lifetime. This book was his autobiography, as told to Thomas D. Bonner. It was titled *The Life and Adventures of James P. Beckwourth, Mountaineer, Scout, and Pioneer, and Chief of the Crow Nation of Indians*. The book opens with his birth in 1798 to a white

Explorer James P. Beckwourth found friends and adventures everywhere he went.

Virginia farmer and a black slave mother, and it details the many twists and turns of his life over the next 50 years. So, yes, a person could learn a lot about the American West from this man who began life as a slave and went on to become a legend in his own time.

3   Of course, some of the stories you would learn might not exactly be true. That is because Beckwourth's life story is a combination of reality and myth. He is partly to blame, since he was always willing to embellish his own adventures. If he and 50 other men were attacked by 50 enemies, Beckwourth might retell the story so that he and just 10 other men were up against 500 enemies. Because of this type of exaggeration, people called him "The Gaudy Liar." This label, however, might be taken either as a slur or a compliment. It was a slur when used by an outsider who was perhaps jealous of Beckwourth's adventures. It was a compliment when used by his partners and the mountain men who shared tall tales with him at their annual winter meeting place. For these men, the biggest sin was being a bore, and no one could accuse Beckwourth of that. All those who heard his stories acknowledged that the man was a master storyteller.

4   Exaggerations aside, the facts of Beckwourth's life are fascinating enough. As a child growing up first in Virginia and then Missouri, Beckwourth fell in love with the outdoor life. When he was a young man, his father gave him his emancipation papers, ending Beckwourth's enslavement.

Still, as an African American from a region where slavery was still in force, Beckwourth felt that a more complete freedom waited for him in the untamed West. He joined a beaver-trapping expedition and headed toward the mountains. There he became an expert marksman and a skilled survivalist.

5   One day in 1828, while out trapping, Beckwourth was captured by Crow warriors. There are several different versions of exactly how this happened, but Beckwourth soon found himself living among the Crow. It turned out to be a good fit. First of all, Beckwourth felt relieved to be away from the racial discrimination he had experienced throughout his life. In time, he gained great influence among the Crow. He joined in many of their battles, rose in status to become a war chief, and married several Crow women. He stayed with the Crow for nearly eight years.

6   Then, in search of new adventure and fame, Beckwourth joined the Missouri Volunteers of the United States Army in their war against the Seminole of Florida.

In 1842, Beckwourth stopped his wandering long enough io start his own trading post and settlement.

He stayed in Florida 10 months, doing a bit of scouting and carrying mail. He found the long periods without adventure to be unbearable, however, so he returned to the West in 1838. "I wanted excitement of some kind," he said—but he didn't care much what kind it was. Beckwourth couldn't even get a thrill by stealing horses from the Seminole. "The Seminole had no horses worth stealing, or I should certainly have exercised my talents for the benefit of the United States."

7   Beckwourth traveled to St. Louis, which was a major city on the edge of the western frontier. This was the place where trappers brought their furs to trade for goods and money. The Mississippi River also brought travelers and provided easy access to the outer settlements. Beckwourth probably came to St. Louis to make connections, make money, find excitement, or all three. He wasn't in town very long before he met up with an old friend named Louis Vasquez who, with a partner, was getting ready to set up trade with the Cheyenne, Arapaho, and Sioux. Vasquez was happy to bring Beckwourth into their plans because of Beckwourth's knowledge of the Native American culture and his close association with the Crow.

Beckwourth was named the group's "agent-in-charge," and he quickly formed a friendly relationship with the Cheyenne that would last for many years.

8   After a time, Beckwourth grew tired of working for Vasquez, so he moved on. He married Luisa Sandoval and started his own trading post, which later grew to become present-day Pueblo, Colorado. However, Beckwourth couldn't settle down for long. For the next several years he moved from one activity to the next. He served as a scout, panned for gold, and spent a good deal of time crisscrossing California. Just before the California Gold Rush in 1849, he discovered a low pass through the Sierra Nevada Mountains that was much easier and safer to cross than the dangerous Donner Pass. He and some friends spent half a year building a road that could be used by gold seekers and settlers bringing their families to the West. The merchants of Marysville, California, paid Beckwourth to guide wagon trains to their town. Two decades later, Beckwourth's trail would become the route over the Sierra Nevada Mountains that was used by the Western Pacific Railroad. The pass, which is a few miles north of Reno, Nevada, is still known as Beckwourth Pass.

9   Jim Beckwourth died in 1866. The details of his death were, like the man himself, obstructed by legend. No one knows for sure how he died, but that didn't keep people from making up stories. According to one, he was poisoned by the Crow when he refused to return to them and become their leader. Others say he was trying to negotiate peace between the Crow and local white settlers when he became ill and died. The Crow treated him as an honored warrior by leaving his body on a platform high in a tree. It gave him a splendid view of the land he had traveled through and helped to shape. ✳

If you have been timed while reading this article, enter your reading time below. Then turn to the Words-per-Minute Table on page 55 and look up your reading speed (words per minute). Enter your reading speed on the graph on page 56.

Reading Time: Lesson 4

_____ : _____
Minutes   Seconds

A Finding the Main Idea

One statement below expresses the main idea of the article. One statement is too general, or too broad. The other statement explains only part of the article; it is too narrow. Label the statements using the following key:

M—Main Idea   **B—Too Broad**   **N—Too Narrow**

_____ 1. Nineteenth-century adventurer Jim Beckwourth was willing to try almost any exciting job, including mountain man, trapper, trader, soldier, scout, and war chief.

_____ 2. During the 19th century, the American West was a fascinating place to be, and Jim Beckwourth's life reflects that excitement.

_____ 3. Among Jim Beckwourth's many achievements was the discovery of a low and relatively easy pass through the Sierra Nevada Mountains.

_____ Score 15 points for a correct M answer.

_____ Score 5 points for each correct B or N answer.

_____ **Total Score**: Finding the Main Idea

B Recalling Facts

How well do you remember the facts in the article? Put an X in the box next to the answer that correctly completes each statement about the article.

1. Jim Beckwourth was born in
   - ☐ a. Virginia in 1798.
   - ☐ b. California in 1798.
   - ☐ c. Missouri in 1838.

2. Beckwourth was made a war chief by the
   - ☐ a. Cherokee tribe.
   - ☐ b. Seminole tribe.
   - ☐ c. Crow tribe.

3. Beckwourth's job with the Missouri Volunteers was
   - ☐ a. planning attacks.
   - ☐ b. scouting and carrying mail.
   - ☐ c. negotiating with the Seminole.

4. One job Beckwourth did <u>not</u> do was
   - ☐ a. explore unknown territory.
   - ☐ b. pan for gold.
   - ☐ c. work on a merchant ship.

5. The Beckwourth Pass leads from
   - ☐ a. Missouri to Arkansas.
   - ☐ b. Nevada to California.
   - ☐ c. California to Oregon.

Score 5 points for each correct answer.

_____ **Total Score**: Recalling Facts

C Making Inferences

When you combine your own experiences and information from a text to draw a conclusion that is not directly stated in that text, you are making an inference. Below are five statements that may or may not be inferences based on information in the article. Label the statements using the following key:

C—Correct Inference   **F—Faulty Inference**

_____ 1. At the time of Beckwourth's birth, if your father was a free man, you were also free.

_____ 2. It was against Crow custom and laws for a man to marry more than one woman in a lifetime.

_____ 3. Jim Beckwourth was unusually skilled at making friends.

_____ 4. The Missouri Volunteers did not care that Beckwourth was an African American.

_____ 5. Jim Beckwourth probably did not do any of the things that he said he did.

Score 5 points for each correct answer.

_____ **Total Score**: Making Inferences

D Using Words Precisely

Each numbered sentence below contains an underlined word or phrase from the article. Following the sentence are three definitions. One definition is closest to the meaning of the underlined word. One definition is opposite or nearly opposite. Label those two definitions using the following key. Do not label the remaining definition.

C—Closest   **O—Opposite or Nearly Opposite**

1. He is partly to blame for his life story being considered part myth, since he was always willing to <u>embellish</u> his own adventures.

_____ a. minimize

_____ b. make more interesting

_____ c. describe

2. People called him "The <u>Gaudy</u> Liar."

_____ a. flashy

_____ b. dull, but tasteful

_____ c. humorous

3. This label that people put upon him, however, might be taken either as a <u>slur</u> or as a compliment.

_____ a. joke

_____ b. insult

_____ c. praise

4. All those who heard his stories <u>acknowledged</u> that the man was a master storyteller.

_____ a. denied

_____ b. forgot

_____ c. admitted

5. The details of his death were, like the man himself, <u>obstructed</u> by legend.

_____ a. made better

_____ b. made clear

_____ c. blocked

_____ Score 3 points for each correct C answer.

_____ Score 2 points for each correct O answer.

_____ **Total Score**: Using Words Precisely

Enter the four total scores in the spaces below, and add them together to find your Reading Comprehension Score. Then record your score on the graph on page 57.

Score	Question Type	Lesson 4
_____	Finding the Main Idea	
_____	Recalling Facts	
_____	Making Inferences	
_____	Using Words Precisely	
_____	**Reading Comprehension Score**	

Author's Approach

Put an X in the box next to the correct answer.

1. Choose the statement below that best describes the author's opinion in paragraph 6.

☐ a. It would be fair to call Jim Beckwourth a lazy person.

☐ b. Jim Beckwourth was willing to help only as long as he found the effort interesting or exciting.

☐ c. Jim Beckwourth was a patriot who would do just about anything to help win the war against the Seminole.

2. The author probably wrote this article in order to

☐ a. reveal how unfairly African Americans were treated during the 19th century.

☐ b. describe the life of an average American during the 19th century.

☐ c. inform the reader about a fascinating man.

3. Which of the following statements from the article best describes Jim Beckwourth?

☐ a. "All those who heard his stories acknowledged that the man was a master storyteller."

☐ b. "The Crow treated him as an honored warrior by leaving his body on a platform high in a tree."

☐ c. "Beckwourth would get bored with one adventure and then move on to the next."

_____ Number of correct answers

Record your personal assessment of your work on the Critical Thinking Chart on page 58.

CRITICAL THINKING

Summarizing and Paraphrasing

Put an X in the box next to the correct answer for questions 1 and 3. Follow the directions provided for question 2.

1. Read the statement from the article below. Then read the paraphrase of that statement. Choose the reason that best tells why the paraphrase does not say the same thing as the statement.

   Statement: Still, as an African American from a region where slavery was still in force, Beckwourth believed that a more complete freedom awaited him in the untamed West.

   Paraphrase: Beckwourth understood that he had to go to the untamed West to be completely free.

   ☐ a. Paraphrase says too much.

   ☐ b. Paraphrase doesn't say enough.

   ☐ c. Paraphrase doesn't agree with the statement.

2. Look for the important ideas and events in paragraph 8. Summarize the paragraph in one or two sentences.

   _____

   _____

   _____

   _____

   _____

   _____

3. Choose the sentence that correctly restates the following sentence from the article: ". . . Beckwourth's life story is a combination of reality and myth."

   ☐ a. While we know some facts about Beckwourth's life, some of his story is fiction.

   ☐ b. Beckwourth is a character who was fictional, even though his story is based on facts.

   ☐ c. We really know very little about the life of Jim Beckwourth.

   _____ Number of correct answers

   Record your personal assessment of your work on the Critical Thinking Chart on page 58.

Critical Thinking

Put an X in the box next to the correct answer for questions 1, 2, and 4. Follow the directions provided for question 3.

1. Which of the following statements from the article is an opinion rather than a fact?

   ☐ a. "One day in 1828, while out trapping, Beckwourth was captured by Crow warriors."

   ☐ b. "Of course, some of the stories you would learn might not exactly be true."

   ☐ c. "Exaggerations aside, the facts of Beckwourth's life are fascinating enough."

2. From what the article told about Jim Beckwourth, you can predict that

   ☐ a. he would tell only the truth in his autobiography.

   ☐ b. his autobiography would be interesting.

   ☐ c. his autobiography would be pretty dull.

3. Reread paragraph 4. Then choose from the letters below to correctly complete the following statement. Write the letters on the lines.

   According to paragraph 4, _____ because _____.

   a. Beckwourth wanted to be free from the limitations of racial discrimination

   b. Beckwourth grew up first in Virginia and then in Missouri

   c. Beckwourth went West as a young man

4. What did you have to do to answer question 3?

   ☐ a. find a cause (why something happened)

   ☐ b. find an opinion (what someone thinks about something)

   ☐ c. find a comparison (how things are the same)

   _____ Number of correct answers

   Record your personal assessment of your work on the Critical Thinking Chart on page 58.

Personal Response

A question I would like answered by Jim Beckwourth is

_____

_____

_____

_____

Self-Assessment

From reading this article, I have learned

_____

_____

_____

_____

_____

_____

_____

_____

CRITICAL THINKING

Diving the Andrea Doria

The Italian luxury liner Andrea Doria *sinks slowly into the sea.*

On the morning of July 30, 2008, Terry DeWolf slipped out of a boat and into the Atlantic Ocean. Then he dove down, down, down. When the 38-year-old scuba diver didn't return after four hours, his companions in the boat knew for certain that what they had feared the most had happened. DeWolf wasn't a rookie; he had been diving for 20 years. But a diver's experience and skill don't always amount to much when the dive site is one of the deepest and most dangerous in the world.

2 What attracted DeWolf and others before and after him was the wreck of the *Andrea Doria*. On a July night in 1956, a dense, swirling fog had reduced visibility along the Atlantic coast. The renowned Italian luxury passenger ship *Andrea Doria* was speeding west on the final leg of its trans-Atlantic voyage. Meanwhile, the *Stockholm*, a Swedish passenger ship, had recently left New York harbor and was traveling east. No one knows for sure how the two ships managed to collide. The accident occurred 50 miles south of Nantucket Island, Massachusetts. It was the smaller *Stockholm* that rammed into the *Andrea Doria*. The bulk of the *Stockholm* penetrated the Italian ship's hull, and for a short time the *Stockholm* was carried along by the *Andrea Doria*. The luxury liner was still speeding ahead, but the combined force of water and forward motion tore the *Stockholm* loose from the *Andrea Doria*, and seawater poured into the gaping hole. For many hours, the ocean consumed the 700-foot long ocean liner, until finally it sank beneath the waves. Fifty-one people died in the collision.

3 Since then, the *Andrea Doria*, motionless on the ocean floor some 200 feet below the surface, has inadvertently claimed several more lives. Terry DeWolf was the 15th scuba diver to perish while exploring the famous Italian wreckage. Two hundred feet might not seem like a great distance. But to a scuba diver, going that deep is a bit like a jet pilot soaring to the edge of outer space. Most recreational divers go no lower than 60 feet beneath the surface. Diving down 200 feet is at the outer limits of what even the most accomplished divers can do. At that depth, the temperature of the water is a bone-chilling 42 degrees. Also, the water pressure is so great that the diver must take great care when surfacing. Coming up too quickly will cause a potentially fatal condition known as "the bends," in which gas bubbles form in the body. Finally, at such great depths, there are shifting water currents as well as clouds of silt, plankton,

The Stockholm *returned under its own power to New York Harbor two days after the collision.*

and algae that limit a diver's vision to about 20 feet. Any equipment failure or malfunction could be life threatening.

4   These dangers actually entice some scuba divers. Some call the *Andrea Doria* wreckage "the Mount Everest of diving." If climbing to the top of Mount Everest is the finest prize in mountaineering, then diving down to explore the *Andrea Doria* is the finest prize in the world of scuba diving.

5   Part of the thrill of "diving the *Andrea Doria*" is retrieving rare crystal and china that lies in the wreckage. Such items certainly have value, but what's more important to fame seekers is that these gifts offer tangible proof that the site was conquered. A lot of divers acknowledge that the bragging rights can't be separated from the adventure. Sally Wahrmann, an expert scuba diver who has made more than 60 dives to the *Andrea Doria* admits "They say it's not a competitive sport, but it is."

6   When a diver reaches the *Andrea Doria*, there is potential trouble everywhere. The wreck is so long that the dark rooms and passageways are like a labyrinth. More than one diver has taken a wrong turn and become badly disoriented. That might have been what happened to Craig Sicola, who swam through the *Andrea Doria* in 1998. Sicola was aware of the extreme dangers of the site, but he was determined to bring back some china. When he got down into the ship's kitchen, he had 23 minutes of air left in his tank. That should have been enough to look around the wreck and return safely to the surface. Apparently, something went wrong. Many believe either the silt blinded him or he became lost. Although Sicola ultimately found his way out of the ship, he was nowhere near the anchor line that would bring him back to the boat waiting on the surface. At that point, he apparently panicked and hit the button on his buoyancy vest. This shot him up to the surface far too rapidly. By the time the rescue swimmers reached him, he was dead from the bends, also known as decompression sickness.

7   Another danger of the *Andrea Doria* dive site comes from the jumble of electrical cables that float around inside the wreck. In 1985 diver John Ormsby got caught up in some of these cables. The more he thrashed around trying to free himself, the more entangled he became. Ormsby died at the site, still wrapped in cables and wires. It took divers two days to cut his body free, and even then they needed bolt cutters to do it.

8   It is not just the competitive explorer who flirts with death by exploring the *Andrea Doria*. David Bright was a very capable diver who had researched dozens of shipwrecks, including the *Titanic* and the Civil War ship *USS Monitor*. He had made 120 dives down to the *Andrea Doria*. In fact, Bright was such an authority on the ship that he had written a book about it. He had also established the Andrea Doria Museum Project, which lent artifacts to various museums. Nonetheless, on July 8, 2006, Bright found himself in a struggle for survival when something went wrong at the site. Bright had been down at the wreckage taking pictures and was trying to return to the surface. It is impossible to know exactly what happened, but somehow he lost control on his way back to the surface. When he came up from the depths too quickly, he knew immediately that he was in trouble. He called out to the surface ship, indicating that he needed help. A diver swam out to him, but by then the decompression sickness was so bad that Bright began losing consciousness. Rescuers got him onto a helicopter and to an emergency room as fast as possible, but the hospital pronounced him dead on arrival.

9   Despite the rising death toll, divers continue to take their chances at the *Andrea Doria*. Captain Dan Crowell runs a charter boat for divers wanting to go to the wreckage site. He sums up the situation as well as anyone. Says Crowell, "On a good day, I could take you down with no problem. But the *Andrea Doria* will give you all the rope you need to hang yourself." ✳

If you have been timed while reading this article, enter your reading time below. Then turn to the Words-per-Minute Table on page 55 and look up your reading speed (words per minute). Enter your reading speed on the graph on page 56.

Reading Time: Lesson 5

_____ : _____
Minutes   *Seconds*

A Finding the Main Idea

One statement below expresses the main idea of the article. One statement is too general, or too broad. The other statement explains only part of the article; it is too narrow. Label the statements using the following key:

M—Main Idea   **B—Too Broad**   **N—Too Narrow**

_____ 1. The Italian ship *Andrea Doria* has been an attraction for divers ever since it sank in 1956, and many divers have died exploring it.

_____ 2. Divers are often attracted by sunken ships such as the *Andrea Doria*, which sank in 1956.

_____ 3. A Swedish ship, the *Stockholm*, rammed into an Italian ship, the *Andrea Doria*, in July 1956, causing the death of 51 people.

_____ Score 15 points for a correct M answer.

_____ Score 5 points for each correct B or N answer.

_____ **Total Score**: Finding the Main Idea

B Recalling Facts

How well do you remember the facts in the article? Put an X in the box next to the answer that correctly completes each statement about the article.

1. The *Andrea Doria* sank in the
   - ☐ a. Atlantic Ocean.
   - ☐ b. Pacific Ocean.
   - ☐ c. Mediterranean Sea.

2. Most recreational divers descend
   - ☐ a. to a depth of 200 feet.
   - ☐ b. at least 150 feet.
   - ☐ c. no farther than 60 feet.

3. A condition called the bends occurs when divers
   - ☐ a. run out of oxygen.
   - ☐ b. rise to the surface too quickly.
   - ☐ c. dive too deep.

4. Diver Craig Sicola died when he
   - ☐ a. surfaced too quickly, not near the waiting boat.
   - ☐ b. became stuck in the kitchen of the ship.
   - ☐ c. got tangled in cables.

5. David Bright dove down to the *Andrea Doria* to
   - ☐ a. take pictures of the wreck.
   - ☐ b. retrieve a piece of china from the ship.
   - ☐ c. try to find out exactly why the ship sank.

_____

Score 5 points for each correct answer.

_____ **Total Score**: Recalling Facts

C Making Inferences

When you combine your own experiences and information from a text to draw a conclusion that is not directly stated in that text, you are making an inference. Below are five statements that may or may not be inferences based on information in the article. Label the statements using the following key:

C—Correct Inference   **F—Faulty Inference**

_____ 1. No one could have survived the collision of the *Stockholm* and the *Andrea Doria*.

_____ 2. Winter is the best time of year to explore the *Andrea Doria*.

_____ 3. Passengers must have enjoyed elegant dinners on the *Andrea Doria*.

_____ 4. A skillful diver should be able to explore the *Andrea Doria* without using an air tank.

_____ 5. Decompression sickness can kill a person within a few hours or less.

Score 5 points for each correct answer.

_____ **Total Score**: Making Inferences

D Using Words Precisely

Each numbered sentence below contains an underlined word or phrase from the article. Following the sentence are three definitions. One definition is closest to the meaning of the underlined word. One definition is opposite or nearly opposite. Label those two definitions using the following key. Do not label the remaining definition.

C—Closest   **O—Opposite or Nearly Opposite**

1. The <u>renowned</u> Italian luxury passenger ship *Andrea Doria* was speeding west on the final leg of its transatlantic voyage.

_____ a. famous

_____ b. popular

_____ c. unknown

2. Since then, the *Andrea Doria*, motionless on the ocean floor some 200 feet below the surface, has <u>inadvertently</u> claimed several more lives.

_____ a. purposely

_____ b. not intentionally

_____ c. continually

3. These dangers actually <u>entice</u> some scuba divers.

_____ a. shock

_____ b. drive back

_____ c. attract

4. Such items certainly have value, but what's more important to fame seekers is that these gifts offer <u>tangible</u> proof that the site was conquered.

_____ a. not able to be sensed

_____ b. valuable

_____ c. touchable, solid

5. The wreck is so long that the dark rooms and passageways are like a <u>labyrinth</u>.

_____ a. hole

_____ b. maze

_____ c. clear path

_____ Score 3 points for each correct C answer.

_____ Score 2 points for each correct O answer.

_____ **Total Score**: Using Words Precisely

Enter the four total scores in the spaces below, and add them together to find your Reading Comprehension Score. Then record your score on the graph on page 57.

Score	Question Type	Lesson 5
_____	Finding the Main Idea	
_____	Recalling Facts	
_____	Making Inferences	
_____	Using Words Precisely	
_____	**Reading Comprehension Score**	

Author's Approach

Put an X in the box next to the correct answer.

1. The main purpose of the first paragraph is to
   - ☐ a. inform the reader that diving to the *Andrea Doria* can be dangerous.
   - ☐ b. inform the reader that Terry DeWolf was an experienced diver.
   - ☐ c. describe the wrecked ship *Andrea Doria*.

2. What is the author's purpose in writing this article?
   - ☐ a. to persuade the reader to dive to the *Andrea Doria*
   - ☐ b. to describe the collision of the *Andrea Doria* and the *Stockholm*
   - ☐ c. to inform the reader about a dangerous challenge that some divers attempt for fun

3. From the statements below, choose the one that you believe the author would agree with.
   - ☐ a. No diver can survive diving to the *Andrea Doria*.
   - ☐ b. Obtaining *Andrea Doria's* crystal and china are definitely worth the risk of diving to the wreck.
   - ☐ c. Divers should not take the dangers of diving to the *Andrea Doria* lightly.

_____ Number of correct answers

Record your personal assessment of your work on the Critical Thinking Chart on page 58.

Summarizing and Paraphrasing

Put an X in the box next to the correct answer for question 1. Follow the directions provided for question 2.

1. Read the statement from the article below. Then read the paraphrase of that statement. Choose the reason that best tells why the paraphrase does not say the same thing as the statement.

   Statement: Coming up too quickly will cause a potentially fatal condition in which gas bubbles form in the body, known as "the bends."

   Paraphrase: If divers come up too quickly, they get the bends, and some divers have died as a result.

   ☐ a. Paraphrase says too much.

   ☐ b. Paraphrase doesn't say enough.

   ☐ c. Paraphrase doesn't agree with the statement.

2. Reread paragraph 5 in the article. Below, write a summary of the paragraph in no more than 25 words.

   _____

   _____

   _____

   _____

   _____

   _____

Reread your summary and decide whether it covers the important ideas in the paragraph. Next, decide how to shorten the summary to 15 words or less without leaving out any essential information. Write this summary below.

_____

_____

_____

_____

_____

_____ Number of correct answers

Record your personal assessment of your work on the Critical Thinking Chart on page 58.

Critical Thinking

Put an X in the box next to the correct answer for questions 1 and 2. Follow the directions provided for the other questions.

1. Which of the following statements from the article is an opinion rather than a fact?

   ☐ a. "They say it's not a competitive sport, but it is."

   ☐ b. "Terry DeWolf was the 15th scuba diver to perish while exploring the famous Italian wreckage."

   ☐ c. "On a July night in 1956, a dense, swirling fog had reduced visibility along the Atlantic coast."

CRITICAL THINKING

2. Considering the attitude and actions of divers as described in this article, you can predict that

☐ a. future divers will be too afraid to dive the *Andrea Doria*.

☐ b. some divers will still dive the *Andrea Doria*.

☐ c. the *Andrea Doria* will soon be closed to divers.

3. Choose from the letters below to correctly complete the following statement. Write the letters on the lines.

In the article, _____ and _____ are alike because they both died of the bends.

a. Craig Sicola

b. John Ormsby

c. David Bright

4. Choose from the letters below to correctly complete the following statement. Write the letters on the lines.

According to the article, _____ caused the *Stockholm* to _____, and the effect was _____.

a. a dense fog

b. the sinking of the *Andrea Doria*

c. crash into the *Andrea Doria*

5. In which paragraph did you find your information or details to answer question 4?

_____

_____ Number of correct answers

Record your personal assessment of your work on the Critical Thinking Chart on page 58.

Personal Response

If you could ask the author of the article one question, what would it be?

_____

_____

_____

_____

Self-Assessment

Which concepts or ideas from the article were difficult to understand?

_____

_____

_____

Which ones were easy to understand?

_____

_____

_____

_____

CRITICAL THINKING

Compare and Contrast

Think about the articles you have read in Unit One. Choose three individuals you read about that you admire most. Write the titles of the articles that tell about them in the first column of the chart below. Use information you learned from the articles to fill in the empty boxes in the chart.

Title	What difficulties did the person have to overcome?	What three adjectives would describe this person best?	How did this person benefit from his or her achievement?

A trailblazer I would most like to travel with is _____. I chose this person because _____

_____

_____

Words-per-Minute Table

Unit One

Directions If you were timed while reading an article, refer to the Reading Time you recorded in the box at the end of the article. Use this words-per-minute table to determine your reading speed for that article. Then plot your reading speed on the graph on page 56.

Lesson	Sample	1	2	3	4	5	
No. of Words	1110	1161	1183	1075	1163	1150	
1:30	740	774	789	717	775	767	90
1:40	666	697	710	645	698	690	100
1:50	605	633	645	586	634	627	110
2:00	555	581	592	538	582	575	120
2:10	512	536	546	496	537	531	130
2:20	476	498	507	461	498	493	140
2:30	444	464	473	430	465	460	150
2:40	416	435	444	403	436	431	160
2:50	392	410	418	379	410	406	170
3:00	370	387	394	358	388	383	180
3:10	351	367	374	339	367	363	190
3:20	333	348	355	323	349	345	200
3:30	317	332	338	307	332	329	210
3:40	303	317	323	293	317	314	220
3:50	290	303	309	280	303	300	230
4:00	278	290	296	269	291	288	240
4:10	266	279	284	258	279	276	250
4:20	256	268	273	248	268	265	260
4:30	247	258	263	239	258	256	270
4:40	238	249	254	230	249	246	280
4:50	230	240	245	222	241	238	290
5:00	222	232	237	215	233	230	300
5:10	215	225	229	208	225	223	310
5:20	208	218	222	202	218	216	320
5:30	202	211	215	195	211	209	330
5:40	196	205	209	190	205	203	340
5:50	190	199	203	184	199	197	350
6:00	185	194	197	179	194	192	360
6:10	180	188	192	174	189	186	370
6:20	175	183	187	170	184	182	380
6:30	171	179	182	165	179	177	390
6:40	167	174	177	161	174	173	400
6:50	162	170	173	157	170	168	410
7:00	159	166	169	154	166	164	420
7:10	155	162	165	150	162	160	430
7:20	151	158	161	147	159	157	440
7:30	148	155	158	143	155	153	450
7:40	145	151	154	140	152	150	460
7:50	142	148	151	137	148	147	470
8:00	139	145	148	134	145	144	480

Minutes and Seconds

Seconds

55

Plotting Your Progress: Reading Speed

Unit One

Directions If you were timed while reading an article, write your words-per-minute rate for that article in the box under the number of the lesson. Then plot your reading speed on the graph by putting a small X on the line directly above the number of the lesson, across from the number of words per minute you read. As you mark your speed for each lesson, graph your progress by drawing a line to connect the Xs.

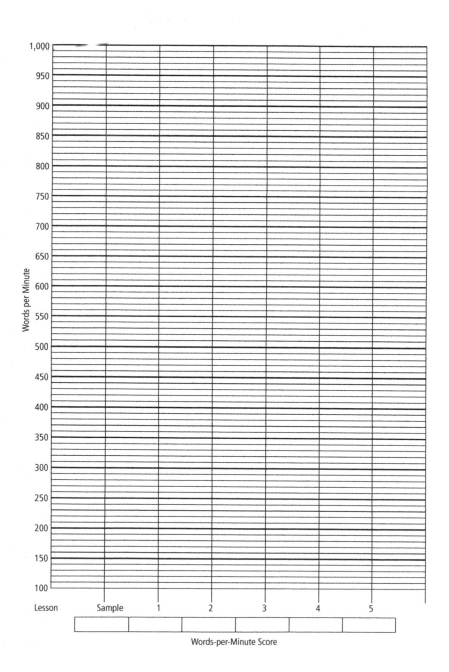

Words-per-Minute Score

Plotting Your Progress: Reading Comprehension

Unit One

Directions Write your Reading Comprehension score for each lesson in the box under the number of the lesson. Then plot your score on the graph by putting a small X on the line directly above the number of the lesson and across from the score you earned. As you mark your score for each lesson, graph your progress by drawing a line to connect the Xs.

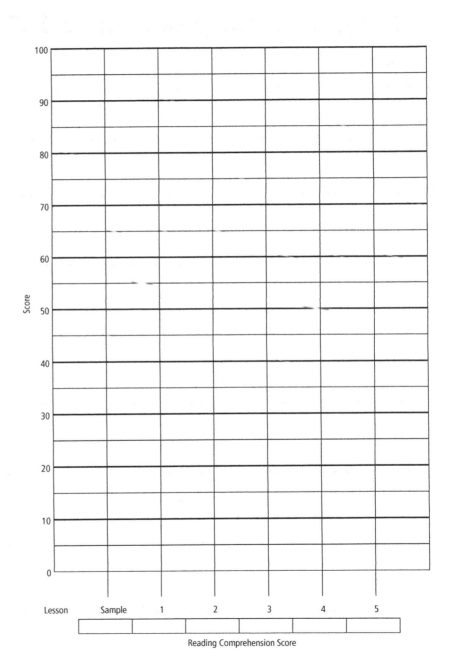

Score

Lesson | Sample | 1 | 2 | 3 | 4 | 5

Reading Comprehension Score

Plotting Your Progress: Critical Thinking

Unit One

Directions Work with your teacher to evaluate your responses to the Critical Thinking questions for each lesson. Then fill in the appropriate spaces in the chart below. For each lesson and each type of Critical Thinking question, do the following: Mark a minus sign (–) in the box to indicate areas in which you feel you could improve. Mark a plus sign (+) to indicate areas in which you feel you did well. Mark a minus-slash-plus sign (–/+) to indicate areas in which you had mixed success. Then write any comments you have about your performance, including ideas for improvement.

Lesson	Author's Approach	Summarizing and Paraphrasing	Critical Thinking
Sample			
1			
2			
3			
4			
5			

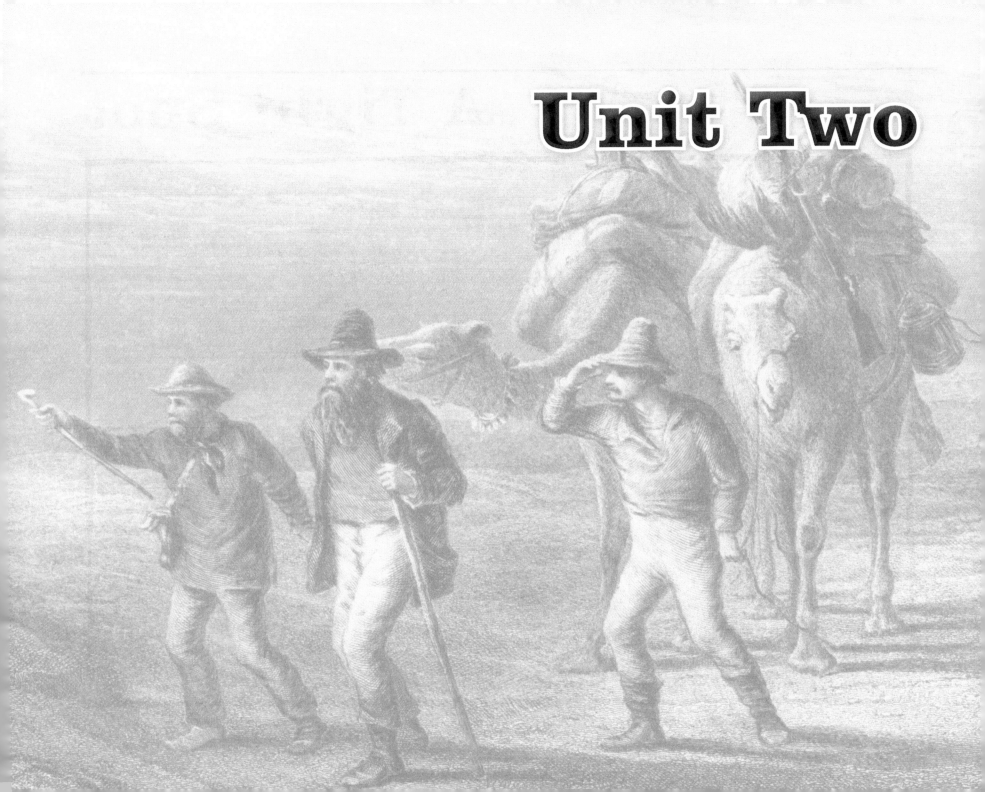

Unit Two

A Tight Spot

This volunteer was part of the rescue effort in Nutty Putty cave, where John Jones became stuck in a passageway.

John Jones was not a wild and crazy guy, but he did enjoy adventures. So when the 26-year-old husband, father, and University of Virginia medical student returned to his native Utah for Thanksgiving vacation, he looked around for something exciting to do. Early in the evening on Tuesday, November 24, 2009, he set off on a spelunking trip with 10 friends and family members. *Spelunking* is the term used for exploring natural caves. This activity was one of Jones's long-time hobbies. Although he was 6 feet tall and weighed 200 pounds, he enjoyed wiggling through damp, narrow passageways, occasionally bumping into a stalagmite or startling a sleeping bat. "We were just looking forward to a good time," his brother Mike recalled.

2   The explorers went to a large, deep cave on the edge of Utah Lake, about 80 miles south of Salt Lake City. The 1,500-foot cave, called Nutty Putty, was popular with cave explorers because it offered a little something for everyone. It featured a large underground room that was easy to reach, and it also contained many difficult tunnels and corridors. The names of some of these passageways add a flavor to the cramped challenges they provide: the Aorta Crawl, the Maze, and Vein Alley. Soon after entering the cave, the group split up. The children and less-experienced spelunkers stayed near the entrance while John Jones and a few others went looking for greater thrills. Farther and farther they crawled, through dark, muddy channels that became progressively tighter. After about two hours, they were 150 feet below the ground and 600 feet away from the cave entrance. "It basically got to a point where we were trying to figure out if the cave went any farther," said Joey Stocking, a member of the group. John Jones, inching along head first, believed it did. "He thought he could kind of keep going on his belly down farther. . . ." recalled Stocking.

3   The passageway that Jones wanted to follow was just 18 inches by 10 inches. In many cases, that sort of tight squeeze would soon open up into a room or larger tunnel. But as it turned out, this particular crevice was simply too small for Jones to get through. He became stuck, wedged in between the narrow walls with his head hanging down at a 70-degree angle and only his feet still visible to the friends behind him.

4   Realizing Jones couldn't free himself, some members of his group returned to the cave entrance to call 911, and Joey Stocking stayed to keep Jones company. While waiting for help to arrive, Jones didn't say much. "I think he was just kind of mentally trying not to freak out about being stuck," said Stocking.

5   By 10 p.m., an hour after Jones first became trapped, rescue crews had arrived on the scene, but they faced a daunting task. Utah County Sherriff's Sergeant Spencer Cannon told reporters that Jones had gotten stuck in "the absolute worst place in the cave." Rescuer Shawn Roundy agreed, saying, "It's very narrow, very awkward, and it's difficult to get rescuers down there." Still, everyone tried to be optimistic. After all, five years earlier a 16-year-old spelunker had gotten stuck in the same exact spot and, although it hadn't been easy, rescuers had gotten him out safely.

6   Throughout the night, workers struggled to fee Jones. Initially, 36 people responded to the 911 call, and eventually

Exploring caves can be challenging, partly because the dangers are concealed by darkness.

more than 100 came to offer their assistance. They took turns jamming themselves down through the small tunnels to where Jones was trapped. Sergeant Cannon remarked on how difficult it was to get around and through the different formations of tunnels in the cave. Hour after hour the rescuers chipped away at the rocky walls, trying to open up enough space to get Jones free.

7   The following day, Wednesday, brought more of the same. All morning and into the afternoon, rescuers worked in shifts, using drills to grind away at the crevice. They also brought in a system of ropes and pulleys in hopes of hoisting Jones out. "His spirits are amazingly good, given the circumstances," reported Sergeant Cannon to the media and family. "Obviously he's very tired; he's very worn out and very uncomfortable. But we're hopeful that once we do get him freed that he's going to be in decent shape." At about 5 p.m., it seemed that progress was finally being made. With the pulleys bolted to the cave walls and the ropes tied around Jones's feet, the rescuers were able to start inching him up through the tight passageway. After pulling him 10 feet, they were able to get food and water to him. They also put through a radio call so that he could talk to his pregnant wife. One of Jones's brothers told a reporter that Jones was holding up remarkably well. "There were periods of panic, disorientation," the brother acknowledged, "but he's in good spirits now."

8   Then, to everyone's shock and horror, the cave wall that was anchoring the pulleys gave way, sending Jones sliding back into the space that had trapped him originally. Once again, he was firmly and completely stuck—and hanging upside down. "We thought he was in the clear, and then we got the news that he had slipped again," said another one of Jones's brothers. "That's when we started to get scared."

9   Jones now faced the prospect of a second night in the dark, this time hanging upside down. His family was familiar enough with caves to know what that meant. With no way for Jones to warm his body, he could die of hypothermia. Another possibility was asphyxiation. Each time he exhaled, his chest compressed just a little, allowing him to slip ever deeper into the tight trap that held him. In time, perhaps, he would not be able to expand his chest enough to fill his lungs with air. Although the rescuers also knew this, they did not give up. As the second evening dragged on, they continued to work feverishly to extricate him. However it became increasingly clear that there weren't very many options left.

Sometime around midnight, after fighting to stay calm and alive for 28 hours, John Jones died, his body still wedged tightly in that small, unyielding niche.

10   At first, officials indicated they would try to bring Jones's body out, but eventually they decided to make the cave his final resting place. There was no point in risking more loss of life in an attempt to retrieve his body. The Nutty Putty cave was closed to the public and a concrete plug was put in the entrance to be sure no one would ever again get inside. The terror that John Jones must have felt would not be experienced by any other person—at least not in the Nutty Putty cave. ✳

If you have been timed while reading this article, enter your reading time below. Then turn to the Words-per-Minute Table on page 101 and look up your reading speed (words per minute). Enter your reading speed on the graph on page 102.

Reading Time: Lesson 6

_____ : _____

Minutes   *Seconds*

A Finding the Main Idea

One statement below expresses the main idea of the article. One statement is too general, or too broad. The other statement explains only part of the article; it is too narrow. Label the statements using the following key:

M—Main Idea   **B—Too Broad**   **N—Too Narrow**

_____ 1. Almost 600 feet from the cave entrance, spelunker John Jones became tightly wedged in a tiny crevice in the Nutty Putty cave in Utah.

_____ 2. Exploring a cave in Utah proved fatal for John Jones when he became wedged in a tight space and could not be rescued.

_____ 3. Although spelunking, or cave exploration, is often fun and challenging, it also includes many risks.

_____ Score 15 points for a correct M answer.

_____ Score 5 points for each correct B or N answer.

_____ **Total Score**: Finding the Main Idea

B Recalling Facts

How well do you remember the facts in the article? Put an X in the box next to the answer that correctly completes each statement about the article.

1. Nutty Putty cave is located in
   - ☐ a. Utah.
   - ☐ b. Nevada.
   - ☐ c. California.

2. John Jones became stuck in a passageway that measured
   - ☐ a. 15 inches by 16 inches.
   - ☐ b. 9 inches by 24 inches.
   - ☐ c. 18 inches by 10 inches.

3. Rescuers used ropes and pulleys to
   - ☐ a. chip away several inches of solid rock.
   - ☐ b. communicate with Jones.
   - ☐ c. pull Jones out a few feet.

4. Jones slipped farther into the crevice each time he
   - ☐ a. moved his head.
   - ☐ b. exhaled.
   - ☐ c. kicked his legs.

5. John Jones died after being trapped for
   - ☐ a. 28 hours.
   - ☐ b. 3 days.
   - ☐ c. 18 hours.

Score 5 points for each correct answer.

_____ **Total Score**: Recalling Facts

C Making Inferences

When you combine your own experiences and information from a text to draw a conclusion that is not directly stated in that text, you are making an inference. Below are five statements that may or may not be inferences based on information in the article. Label the statements using the following key:

C—Correct Inference   **F—Faulty Inference**

_____ 1. Most people who visit caves do not try to explore the most narrow passageways.

_____ 2. The cave was officially closed to the public after Jones died because it had become the resting place for his remains.

_____ 3. Only a few of Jones's relatives and close friends ever heard that he had become stuck in the cave.

_____ 4. Rescue officials were sure that Jones would get out alive, and they were all surprised when he died in the cave.

_____ 5. John Jones was a fearless cave explorer who didn't mind entering small spaces.

Score 5 points for each correct answer.

_____ **Total Score:** Making Inferences

D Using Words Precisely

Each numbered sentence below contains an underlined word or phrase from the article. Following the sentence are three definitions. One definition is closest to the meaning of the underlined word. One definition is opposite or nearly opposite. Label those two definitions using the following key. Do not label the remaining definition.

C—Closest   **O—Opposite or Nearly Opposite**

1. By 10 p.m., an hour after Jones first became trapped, rescue crews had arrived on the scene, but they faced a <u>daunting</u> task.

_____ a. familiar, well-known

_____ b. discouraging, overwhelming

_____ c. comforting, reassuring

2. Still, everyone tried to be <u>optimistic</u>.

_____ a. not confident

_____ b. hopeful

_____ c. helpful

3. "There were periods of panic, <u>disorientation</u>," the brother acknowledged, "but he's in good spirits now."

_____ a. clearness

_____ b. anger

_____ c. confusion

4. As the second evening dragged on, they continued to work feverishly to <u>extricate</u> him.

_____ a. release

_____ b. trap

_____ c. comfort

5. Sometime around midnight, after fighting to stay calm and alive for 28 hours, John Jones died, his body still wedged tightly in that small, <u>unyielding</u> niche.

_____ a. uncomfortable

_____ b. bending easily, soft

_____ c. not flexible, stubborn

_____ Score 3 points for each correct C answer.

_____ Score 2 points for each correct O answer.

_____ **Total Score**: Using Words Precisely

Enter the four total scores in the spaces below, and add them together to find your Reading Comprehension Score. Then record your score on the graph on page 103.

Score	Question Type	Lesson 6
_____	Finding the Main Idea	
_____	Recalling Facts	
_____	Making Inferences	
_____	Using Words Precisely	
_____	**Reading Comprehension Score**	

Author's Approach

Put an X in the box next to the correct answer.

1. The main purpose of the first paragraph is to

☐ a. persuade readers to try cave exploration.

☐ b. introduce the characters and setting of the story.

☐ c. define the word *spelunking*.

2. Choose the statement below that best describes the author's opinion in paragraph 10.

☐ a. The decision to leave Jones in the cave was cowardly.

☐ b. Leaving Jones in the cave was cruel to his family.

☐ c. The decision to leave Jones in the cave was sensible.

3. Considering the statement from the article "His spirits are amazingly good, given the circumstances," you can conclude that the author wants the reader to think that

☐ a. Jones maintained a positive attitude in the face of adversity.

☐ b. Jones didn't think he was really in danger at all.

☐ c. most people in that situation would have reacted the same way Jones did.

4. In this article, "The 1,500-foot cave, called Nutty Putty, was popular with cave explorers because it offered a little something for everyone" means

☐ a. the cave offered many options for exploring.

☐ b. although the cave was small, most cave explorers still liked it.

☐ c. people could do other things besides explore Nutty Putty.

_____ Number of correct answers

Record your personal assessment of your work on the Critical Thinking Chart on page 104.

CRITICAL THINKING

Summarizing and Paraphrasing

Put an X in the box next to the correct answer for question 1. Follow the directions provided for questions 2 and 3.

1. Choose the best one-sentence paraphrase for the following sentence from the article: "Initially, 36 people responded to the 911 call, and eventually more than 100 came to offer their assistance."

☐ a. Although only 36 people heard the 911 call, more than 100 people came to help.

☐ b. At first, more than 100 people offered to help, but by the end only 36 people remained.

☐ c. At first, the 911 call brought in 36 people, and before the ordeal ended, more than 100 had shown up to help.

2. Complete the following one-sentence summary of the article using the lettered phrases from the phrase bank below. Write the letters on the lines.

> **Phrase Bank:**
> a. a description of Jones and how he became trapped
> b. the decision to leave Jones's body in the cave
> c. the efforts to free Jones and their outcome

The article, "A Tight Spot," begins with _____, goes on to describe _____, and ends with _____.

3. Look for the important ideas and events in paragraphs 7 and 8. Summarize those paragraphs in one or two sentences.

_____
_____
_____
_____

_____ Number of correct answers

Record your personal assessment of your work on the Critical Thinking Chart on page 104.

Critical Thinking

Follow the directions provided for question 1. Put an X next to the correct answer for the other questions.

1. For each statement below, write O if it expresses an opinion or write F if it expresses a fact.

_____ a. John Jones died sometime after midnight on November 26, 2009.

_____ b. Jones was too heavy and tall to be a spelunker.

_____ c. Nutty Putty is on the edge of Utah Lake.

2. From the article, you can predict that

☐ a. most people who witnessed Jones's ordeal will become interesting in spelunking as a hobby.

☐ b. Jones's friends will never again explore another cave.

☐ c. Nutty Putty will stay off-limits to the public for years.

3. What was the effect of the cave wall giving way?

☐ a. Jones slipped back into the narrow passage.

☐ b. Jones was able to talk to his wife.

☐ c. Rescuers were able to widen the narrow passageway that trapped Jones.

4. How is John Jones an example of the theme of *Trailblazers*?

☐ a. Jones was the first person to explore Nutty Putty.

☐ b. Jones tried to discover a part of the cave no one had ever seen before.

☐ c. Jones was willing to take risks to enjoy his hobby.

5. Judging by events in the article, you can conclude that

☐ a. many people are willing to help a stranger in need.

☐ b. whenever you attempt something dangerous, someone will always be available to help if needed.

☐ c. if you explore a cave with friends, you will be safe.

_____ Number of correct answers

Record your personal assessment of your work on the Critical Thinking Chart on page 104.

Personal Response

I can't believe

_____

_____

_____

_____

Self-Assessment

When reading the article, I was having trouble with

_____

_____

_____

_____

_____

_____

_____

_____

No Second Chances

Cheryl Stearns has completed more skydives than any other woman in history.

W hat would you say about someone who sits in the open cockpit of a small biplane and asks the pilot to deliberately flip the plane upside down so she can unfasten her seatbelt and tumble out into space? You'd probably think this person was a little—well, *unusual,* at least. But this kind of behavior is quite normal for Cheryl Stearns, the most decorated parachutist in history. She was just having some fun by adding a bit of spice to one of her 17,000 parachute jumps.

2   As a child growing up in the 1960s, Cheryl Stearns often dreamed that she could fly. So she did not surprise anyone when, at the age of 17, she asked to borrow $40 from her parents to enroll in a one-day parachuting class in order to experience the real thing. Her parents, hoping this class would satisfy her urge to fly, reluctantly gave her the money and signed the required permission slip. Stearns says she intended to quit after making one jump, but of course it didn't work out that way. Once she experienced the sensation of skydiving, she was hooked for life.

3   By age 19, Stearns had decided that she wanted to become a competitive skydiver. She contacted a world-famous skydiving coach named Gene Thacker who ran a

skydiving center in North Carolina. Stearns asked if he would teach her the right techniques. Recalls Thacker, "What really impressed me about her, what made me encourage her, was that at 19 she already had a couple of years of college, many job experiences, and had gotten a pilot's license with a commercial rating." Anyone with those credentials, he thought, had to have a lot of ambition.

4   For the next couple of years, Stearns worked for Thacker. She helped him maintain his aircraft and pack parachutes for his jumpers. In return, he helped Stearns hone her skills in the classic traits of competitive parachuting—style and accuracy. Style points are earned by making a series of six turns and back loops as quickly as possible. Accuracy points are won by landing so that one heel touches a target about the size of a silver dollar.

5   Stearns trained hard, jumping six times a day, seven days a week. In 1977 she took the competitive skydiving world by storm, winning her first national skydiving championship and establishing a new world record for accuracy. That year she also joined the United States Army and became the first female member of the Golden Knights. This excellent parachuting team had dominated national and international competition for three decades. As a Golden Knight, Stearns often had the thrill of parachuting into football stadiums. In 1983 she became the national overall military parachuting champion, the first woman ever to win this title.

6   Stearns has never considered herself a daredevil. As she points out, she tries hard to eliminate all unnecessary risks and is meticulous about caring for her equipment. In addition, she typically opens her chute around 2,500 feet, a higher altitude than many other jumpers do. "If I have a malfunction, I want to have those extra 500 feet to deal with the emergency," she says. "Remember, I can always lose altitude, but I can never gain it back."

7   No matter how much care she takes, there remains an element of risk in every skydive she makes. In fact, skydiving is sometimes called taking "a leap of faith." The parachutist is entrusting his or her life to the equipment. If the primary chute doesn't open, a jumper has just a few seconds to deploy the reserve chute. Otherwise, there's nothing else between the jumper and the ground. On one of Stearns's many jumps, her main chute failed to open

Stearns's free-fall from 24 miles above Earth will benefit scientific research.

properly when she pulled her ripcord. Luckily, having rehearsed for this potential catastrophe, she knew what to do. First, she did a mid-air flip so that her back was toward the ground and her stomach was facing up. She was wearing her reserve chute on her stomach, so this position allowed the reserve chute to open freely when she activated it. Stearns estimates that she was no more than 200 to 300 feet above the ground when the reserve chute opened fully. "When I got on the ground I absolutely lost it," she said. "I just stood there and said, 'you almost killed yourself, you almost killed yourself!' If I had waited one more second to pull, I would have impacted."

8   Stearns says the keys to her success are preparation and practice. Success certainly has fed her self-confidence, but too much confidence also can be a bad thing. Stearns does not deny her fear when she is about to jump. In other words, for people who parachute, fear should be a factor. Fear helps Stearns to stay aware of the danger, and this awareness helps keep her mind ready to solve problems that might occur in midair. "This is a very unforgiving sport," Stearns says. "All it takes is one."

9   Over her long jumping career, Stearns has set dozens of world parachuting records. She has also won more than 70 women's titles at national and international championships. Stearns has even been awarded the most prestigious international prize for skydivers: the Leonardo da Vinci diploma. Perhaps the highlight of her career was her astonishing performance on December 9, 1995, when she set the record for the most jumps by anyone in one 24-hour period. During those hours of continuous skydiving, she made a total of 352 jumps. That's one jump for every 4.09 minutes, for 24 straight hours! To accomplish this feat, Stearns needed the help of more than 150 dedicated and highly skilled volunteers. They performed many essential tasks, from piloting the planes to packing the chutes. Driven by her incredible competitive urge, Stearns wasn't content simply to make a record number of jumps; she wanted them to be precision jumps. Of her 352 jumps, she scored a record number of "bull's eye" landings, hitting the center of the landing target 188 times. In the process, she set a new nighttime record of 84 perfect landings.

10   What can Cheryl Stearns do for an encore? She's planning to compete for the high-altitude record. To accomplish this, Stearns will pilot a hot-air balloon high up into the sky until she reaches the far edge of Earth's stratosphere. Because oxygen is so thin at that height, she will have to wear something similar to a space suit. Then, when she is ready, she will dive over the side, with her body in the shape of a spear—head first and arms at her side. Her daring fall will take about 3.5 minutes, during which time she will travel 105,000 feet at about 900 miles per hour. She might even become the first person without a vehicle to break the speed of sound! Stearns has already begun to prepare for the jump of her life. "If I'm not in the proper position . . . I hate to use the word *disintegrate*, but I could be in real trouble." ✳

If you have been timed while reading this article, enter your reading time below. Then turn to the Words-per-Minute Table on page 101 and look up your reading speed (words per minute). Enter your reading speed on the graph on page 102.

Reading Time: Lesson 7

_____ : _____
Minutes   *Seconds*

A Finding the Main Idea

One statement below expresses the main idea of the article. One statement is too general, or too broad. The other statement explains only part of the article; it is too narrow. Label the statements using the following key:

M—Main Idea   **B—Too Broad**   **N—Too Narrow**

_____ 1. Through hard work, Cheryl Stearns has earned a reputation as a daring, skillful, world-class parachutist.

_____ 2. Parachuting is a popular and yet potentially dangerous sport.

_____ 3. Cheryl Stearns started her career in parachuting at the age of 17, when she took her first parachuting class.

_____ Score 15 points for a correct M answer.

_____ Score 5 points for each correct B or N answer.

_____ **Total Score**: Finding the Main Idea

B Recalling Facts

How well do you remember the facts in the article? Put an X in the box next to the answer that correctly completes each statement about the article.

1. Cheryl Stearns got her early training in parachuting from
   - ☐ a. an experienced pilot near her home.
   - ☐ b. instructors in the United States Army.
   - ☐ c. skydiving coach Gene Thacker.

2. Accuracy points are awarded if the parachutist's heel lands on
   - ☐ a. a target the size of a silver dollar.
   - ☐ b. a target about as large as a small pizza.
   - ☐ c. a target the size of a child's wading pool.

3. Usually Cheryl Stearns opens her chute at about
   - ☐ a. 2,500 feet.
   - ☐ b. 500 feet.
   - ☐ c. 250 feet.

4. To set the record for the most jumps in a 24-hour period, Cheryl Stearns jumped
   - ☐ a. 24 times.
   - ☐ b. 100 times.
   - ☐ c. 352 times.

5. Cheryl Stearns hopes to set a record by performing the
   - ☐ a. first jump from a space shuttle.
   - ☐ b. highest parachute jump ever.
   - ☐ c. most parachute jumps in a week.

Score 5 points for each correct answer.

_____ **Total Score**: Recalling Facts

C Making Inferences

When you combine your own experiences and information from a text to draw a conclusion that is not directly stated in that text, you are making an inference. Below are five statements that may or may not be inferences based on information in the article. Label the statements using the following key:

C—Correct Inference   **F—Faulty Inference**

_____ 1. By the age of 19, few people have finished a couple of years of college, earned a pilot's license, and worked a few jobs.

_____ 2. Parachutists are never allowed to jump after sundown.

_____ 3. Cheryl Stearns will have no fear when she tries for her record jump from the hot-air balloon.

_____ 4. Inspecting and packing parachutes carefully is an important job.

_____ 5. It is crucial that parachutists be able to think and react quickly.

Score 5 points for each correct answer.

_____ **Total Score**: Making Inferences

D Using Words Precisely

Each numbered sentence below contains an underlined word or phrase from the article. Following the sentence are three definitions. One definition is closest to the meaning of the underlined word. One definition is opposite or nearly opposite. Label those two definitions using the following key. Do not label the remaining definition.

C—Closest   **O—Opposite or Nearly Opposite**

1. In return, he helped Stearns <u>hone</u> her skills in the classic traits of competitive parachuting—style and accuracy.

_____ a. define

_____ b. worsen

_____ c. make more perfect

2. This excellent parachuting team had <u>dominated</u> national and international competition for three decades.

_____ a. controlled or reigned over

_____ b. shown lesser power or strength

_____ c. accepted eagerly

3. As she points out, she tries hard to eliminate all unnecessary risks and is <u>meticulous</u> about caring for her equipment.

_____ a. hopeful

_____ b. extremely careful

_____ c. sloppy

4. "If I have a <u>malfunction</u>, I want to have those extra 500 feet to deal with the emergency," she says.

_____ a. situation in which things work perfectly

_____ b. failure in equipment

_____ c. shocking situation

5. Stearns has even been awarded the most <u>prestigious</u> international prize for skydivers: the Leonardo da Vinci diploma.

_____ a. honored, highly respected

_____ b. disgraceful and scorned

_____ c. elegant or stylish

_____ Score 3 points for each correct C answer.

_____ Score 2 points for each correct O answer.

_____ **Total Score**: Using Words Precisely

Enter the four total scores in the spaces below, and add them together to find your Reading Comprehension Score. Then record your score on the graph on page 103.

Score	Question Type	Lesson 7
_____	Finding the Main Idea	
_____	Recalling Facts	
_____	Making Inferences	
_____	Using Words Precisely	
_____	**Reading Comprehension Score**	

Author's Approach

Put an X in the box next to the correct answer.

1. The author uses the first sentence of the article to
   - [ ] a. describe the way most parachutists prepare to jump.
   - [ ] b. impress the reader with Cheryl Stearns's willingness to take a risk.
   - [ ] c. show that Cheryl Stearns plans her jumps carefully.

2. What is the author's purpose in writing this article?
   - [ ] a. to persuade the reader to try parachuting
   - [ ] b. to express an opinion about parachuting
   - [ ] c. to inform the reader about a fascinating athlete

3. Choose the statement below that is the weakest argument for parachuting.
   - [ ] a. Parachuting provides a thrill.
   - [ ] b. A parachuting accident can be avoided if you are careful.
   - [ ] c. Parachuting is a great personal challenge.

4. In this article, "All it takes is one" means
   - [ ] a. in parachuting, one mistake can kill you.
   - [ ] b. parachuting demands that each person think for himself or herself.
   - [ ] c. just one person can be the best at parachuting.

_____ Number of correct answers

Record your personal assessment of your work on the Critical Thinking Chart on page 104.

Summarizing and Paraphrasing

Put an X in the box next to the correct answer for question 1. Follow the directions provided for question 2.

1. Choose the best one-sentence paraphrase for the following sentence from the article: "Once she experienced the sensation of skydiving, she was hooked for life."

    ☐ a. The sensation of skydiving was so unusual that she had to try it one more time.

    ☐ b. Skydiving can make you feel so good that you will want to talk about it to everyone in your life.

    ☐ c. After she felt what it was like to skydive, she couldn't stay away from it from then on.

2. Complete the following one-sentence summary of the article using the lettered phrases from the phrase bank below. Write the letters on the lines.

Phrase Bank:

a. Stearns's accomplishments throughout her career

b. Stearns's introduction to and training in parachuting

c. Stearns's plans for the future

The article "No Second Chances" begins with _____, goes on to describe _____, and ends with _____.

_____ Number of correct answers

Record your personal assessment of your work on the Critical Thinking Chart on page 104.

Critical Thinking

Put an X in the box next to the correct answer for questions 1 and 4. Follow the directions provided for the other questions.

1. From the article, you can predict that if Cheryl Stearns gets the funding for her new project,

    ☐ a. she will use the money to fund a different, more exciting parachute stunt.

    ☐ b. she will be ready and eager to try it.

    ☐ c. no one will care if she completes the project or not.

2. Choose from the letters below to correctly complete the following statement. Write the letters on the lines.

    On the positive side, _____, but on the negative side _____.

    a. Stearns is good at her job and loves it

    b. the job Stearns has chosen is quite dangerous

    c. Stearns does not consider herself to be a daredevil

3. Think about cause-effect relationships in the article. Fill in the blanks in the cause-effect chart, drawing from the letters below.

Cause	Effect
She tried parachuting once.	_____
_____	She impressed Thacker.
Her main parachute failed.	_____

    a. Stearns had to flip over and activate her reserve chute.

    b. Stearns became hooked on parachuting.

    c. Stearns showed unusual determination as a teen.

4. How is Cheryl Stearns an example of a Trailblazer?

☐ a. She does things no one has done before.

☐ b. She is willing to accept challenges.

☐ c. She is a careful planner who tries to eliminate risks.

5. Which paragraphs provide evidence that supports your answers to question 3?

_____

_____ Number of correct answers

Record your personal assessment of your work on the Critical Thinking Chart on page 104.

Personal Response

Begin the first 5 to 8 sentences of your own article about a risky activity such as parachuting. It may tell of a real experience or one that is imagined.

_____

_____

_____

_____

_____

_____

Self-Assessment

One of the things I did best when reading this article was

_____

_____

_____

_____

_____

_____

_____

I believe I did this well because

_____

_____

_____

_____

_____

_____

CRITICAL THINKING

Burke and Wills

First Across the Continent

Robert Burke and William Wills had very little knowledge of the Australian interior before they chose to cross it.

It sounded like a grand and exotic adventure. Robert Burke would leave Melbourne, Australia, and head north across the interior of the continent until he reached the coast on the other side. As he set out to explore this vast expanse of uncharted wilderness, no one knew what he might find. Britain had claimed the entire continent for itself, but at the time— the spring of 1860—Europeans knew less about the interior of Australia than is known today about the surface of Mars. The European immigrant population stayed close to the edges of the continent, where fishing and water transportation were available. Only the native people, called Aborigines, were willing to travel inland. Robert Burke pledged to end the mystery of what or who lived in the interior, declaring, "I will cross Australia or perish in the attempt." He had no way of knowing how close to the truth he was.

2   Despite Burke's courageous intentions, he had no real qualifications as an explorer. Born in Ireland, Burke was a police officer by training and had never before ventured into "the bush," as the interior region of Australia was known then. The supplies he ordered for the trip reflected his inexperience. Burke started out with 20 tons of supplies, including everything from cedar-topped dining tables to small brushes designed to keep dandruff off his uniform. William Wills, who was his faithful second-in-command, had been a land surveyor, but he too was completely unprepared for the hardships that awaited them.

3   Burke and Wills began their journey on August 20, 1860, setting out with 19 men, 23 horses, and two dozen camels. The camels had been imported from Pakistan because they were good pack animals, especially for the trek across the dry interior. Right from the start, the expedition struggled. There was a road leading north from Melbourne to the last European settlement of Menindie, 466 miles away, but Burke preferred to blaze his own trail. Consequently, the group's progress was painfully slow. When the terrain was boggy, the camels stumbled; when it was sandy, the horses floundered. It took the expedition nearly two months to reach Menindie. By then, several men had deserted, and all the animals were leg-weary. And that stretch was the easy part of the trip.

4   In Menindie, Burke divided the expedition to make faster progress. He ordered the main group to carry the bulk of the provisions while he, Wills, and six others went ahead with the only the bare necessities. Burke's advance group journeyed hundreds of miles across plains and through swamps to a place called Cooper's Creek. There they set up a camp and waited for the others to join them. Six weeks passed,

however, and no one appeared. Frustrated and out of patience, Burke decided to split the group again. On December 16, 1860, he left four men at Cooper's Creek while he and Wills headed north with John King and Charley Grey. They took six camels and one horse with them. To get to the coast and back, they would have to cover about 1,900 miles. Burke was sure they could do it in 12 weeks, so he packed food and supplies based on that estimate. He also gave orders for the remaining men at Cooper's Creek to wait three months and then head back to Menindie. He told them that if he was not back by then, they could assume he had not survived the journey.

5   It is hard to know how Burke calculated the 12-week estimate, but it turned out to be

Australia's vast interior, also known as the Outback, is mainly rough, undeveloped land made up of deserts, mountains, and scrub brush.

terribly inaccurate. After leaving Cooper's Creek, Burke and his three companions encountered a wide desert, where daytime temperatures soared above 100 degrees. The hot, dry wind blew sand in their eyes, and the ground was littered with sharp rocks. After pushing through the desert, the group faced a forbidding mountain range of steep slopes and deep ravines. Soon, Burke wrote in his journal, the camels were "sweating profusely from fear."

6   By the time the men descended out of the mountains, six weeks had passed, half of their food supply was gone, and they were still 125 miles from the coast. Yet Burke would not abandon his mission. With the rainy season setting in, the group had to trudge through heavy thunderstorms and torrential rains. The camels, worn out from the mountains, struggled in the mud, sloshing through floodwaters that came almost to their knees.

7   Seven weeks after leaving Cooper's Creek, Burke was desperate enough to try something audacious. He split his party for the third time, leaving King and Grey with the camels while he and Wills made one last frenzied trek for the coast. When they came upon a saltwater creek, they knew they were close, yet they still could not see the ocean. At last, on February 9, they stepped into a mangrove swamp so dense and tangled that they could not penetrate it. They had no choice then but to turn back. Burke and Wills were just 12 miles from the northern coast.

8   Bitterly disappointed, the two explorers retraced their path back to John King and Charley Grey, and then the four men began the long walk back toward Cooper's Creek. However, their food was running out, so Burke put them all on starvation rations. Tired, hungry, and completely dispirited, with the animals in pitiful condition, they made very slow progress. As they slogged through the bogs, over the mountains, and into the scorching desert, they grew progressively weaker. On March 25, Wills caught Charley Grey stealing food from the group's rations. Burke lost control and gave Grey a furious beating. A few days later, the group began slaughtering the camels for meat, and eventually they killed the horse as well. The meat came too late to save Grey, who died on April 16. Burke and Wills spent an entire day digging his grave and preparing a proper burial. The trio set off again, and finally made it back into the Cooper's Creek camp.

9   Call it irony, call it tragedy, or call it simply bad luck, but the day spent burying Charley Grey sealed the explorers' fate. The men who had been left behind at Cooper's Creek had waited long past the three-month mark for their leaders to return, and after four months and five days, they left. But it was just eight hours before Burke, Wills, and King returned that the men at Cooper's Creek abandoned the camp and headed home, taking most of their supplies and all of their animals with them. When the three emaciated explorers finally stumbled into the camp, they learned what they probably had feared. After resting a couple of days, Burke, Wills, and King buried their journals under a tree and continued southward, though they were too weak to get very far. They tried to survive on grass seeds and dead rats, but it was not enough. In late June, both Burke and Wills died of starvation. John King was saved by generous Aborigines and was found by a search party three months later.

10   When the buried journals were found, they revealed to the outside world the harsh complexities of the Australian interior. Beyond that, the explorers' heroic determination touched people's hearts. In the eyes of many Australians, Robert Burke and William Wills belong among the ranks of the world's greatest explorers. ✳

If you have been timed while reading this article, enter your reading time below. Then turn to the Words-per-Minute Table on page 101 and look up your reading speed (words per minute). Enter your reading speed on the graph on page 102.

Reading Time: Lesson 8

_____ : _____
Minutes   *Seconds*

A | Finding the Main Idea

One statement below expresses the main idea of the article. One statement is too general, or too broad. The other statement explains only part of the article; it is too narrow. Label the statements using the following key:

M—Main Idea   **B—Too Broad**   **N—Too Narrow**

_____ 1. In 1860 the interior of the Australian continent was an uncharted wilderness.

_____ 2. Robert Burke brought 20 tons of supplies on his journey to explore the interior of Australia.

_____ 3. In 1860 Robert Burke and William Wills led a group of men exploring the interior of Australia but met with tragedy and death.

_____ Score 15 points for a correct M answer.

_____ Score 5 points for each correct B or N answer.

_____ **Total Score**: Finding the Main Idea

B | Recalling Facts

How well do you remember the facts in the article? Put an X in the box next to the answer that correctly completes each statement about the article.

1. Before his expedition in Australia, Robert Burke had been
   ☐ a. an explorer.
   ☐ b. a land surveyor.
   ☐ c. a police officer.

2. Burke imported camels from
   ☐ a. Pakistan.
   ☐ b. Egypt.
   ☐ c. Iraq.

3. Burke started his expedition in the city of
   ☐ a. Menindie.
   ☐ b. Melbourne.
   ☐ c. Cooper's Creek.

4. Burke told the men at the camp to wait for his return for
   ☐ a. three months.
   ☐ b. six weeks.
   ☐ c. two months.

5. The explorer who was saved by Aborigines was
   ☐ a. Charley Grey.
   ☐ b. William Wills.
   ☐ c. John King.

Score 5 points for each correct answer.

_____ **Total Score**: Recalling Facts

C Making Inferences

When you combine your own experiences and information from a text to draw a conclusion that is not directly stated in that text, you are making an inference. Below are five statements that may or may not be inferences based on information in the article. Label the statements using the following key:

C—Correct Inference   F—Faulty Inference

_____ 1. The interior of Australia turned out to be a lot harsher than Burke expected.

_____ 2. Despite telling his men at the camp to leave if he did not return, Burke hoped they would stay until he came back.

_____ 3. Burke and his companions buried their journals because they did not want anyone to read them.

_____ 4. Robert Burke was a strong-willed man.

_____ 5. After Burke's notes were found and publicized, no further exploration of the interior of Australia was needed.

Score 5 points for each correct answer.

_____ **Total Score**: Making Inferences

D Using Words Precisely

Each numbered sentence below contains an underlined word or phrase from the article. Following the sentence are three definitions. One definition is closest to the meaning of the underlined word. One definition is opposite or nearly opposite. Label those two definitions using the following key. Do not label the remaining definition.

C—Closest   O—Opposite or Nearly Opposite

1. When the terrain was boggy, the camels stumbled; when it was sandy, the horses floundered.

_____ a. gripped, gained traction

_____ b. slipped, faltered

_____ c. sweated

2. Soon, Burke wrote in his journal, the camels were "sweating profusely from fear."

_____ a. in great abundance

_____ b. painfully

_____ c. barely adequately

3. Burke was desperate enough to try something audacious.

_____ a. cautious

_____ b. new

_____ c. recklessly daring, bold

4. The explorers made one last frenzied trek for the coast.

_____ a. calm, controlled

_____ b. furious, wild

_____ c. hopeless

5. The four men were tired, hungry, and completely <u>dispirited</u>.

_____ a. exhausted

_____ b. happy, enthusiastic

_____ c. gloomy, discouraged

_____ Score 3 points for each correct C answer.

_____ Score 2 points for each correct O answer.

_____ **Total Score**: Using Words Precisely

Enter the four total scores in the spaces below, and add them together to find your Reading Comprehension Score. Then record your score on the graph on page 103.

Score	Question Type	Lesson 8
_____	Finding the Main Idea	
_____	Recalling Facts	
_____	Making Inferences	
_____	Using Words Precisely	
_____	**Reading Comprehension Score**	

Author's Approach

Put an X in the box next to the correct answer.

1. What is the author's purpose in writing this article?

☐ a. to encourage the reader to learn more about Australia

☐ b. to inform the reader about a historical event

☐ c. to describe the geography of the Australian interior

2. From the statements below, choose two that you believe the author would agree with most strongly.

☐ a. The supplies that Burke chose for the expedition included many unnecessary and foolish items.

☐ b. The interior of Australia is not worth exploring.

☐ c. The expedition ended in tragedy due to Burke's many poor decisions as well as bad luck.

3. The author tells this story mainly by

☐ a. guessing what happened on the expedition, since most of the men died on the journey.

☐ b. describing physical features of the Australian interior.

☐ c. relating events of the trip in the order they happened.

4. Considering the statement from the article "It is hard to know how Burke calculated the 12-week estimate, but it turned out to be terribly inaccurate" you can conclude that the author wants the reader to think that

☐ a. Burke's method of calculation was faulty.

☐ b. Burke simply guessed at the number of weeks he needed.

☐ c. Burke estimated correctly, but other factors delayed him.

_____ Number of correct answers

Record your personal assessment of your work on the Critical Thinking Chart on page 104.

Summarizing and Paraphrasing

Put an X in the box next to the correct answer for questions 1 and 2. Follow the directions provided for question 3.

1. Choose the best one-sentence paraphrase for the following sentence from the article: "In the eyes of many Australians, Robert Burke and William Wills belong among the ranks of the world's greatest explorers."

☐ a. Many Australians consider Burke and Wills to be two of the best trailblazers that ever lived.

☐ b. Most Australians think Burke and Wills are the world's greatest pioneers.

☐ c. Many Australians admire Burke and Wills because they are the world's two most important explorers.

2. Read the statement about the explorers from the article below. Then read the paraphrase of that statement. Choose the reason that best tells why the paraphrase does not say the same thing as the statement.

Statement: The explorers' heroic determination touched people's hearts.

Paraphrase: The actions of these heroes inspired people.

☐ a. Paraphrase says too much.

☐ b. Paraphrase doesn't say enough.

☐ c. Paraphrase doesn't agree with the statement.

3. Reread paragraph 2 in the article. Below, write a summary of the paragraph in no more than 25 words.

_____

_____

_____

_____

_____

Reread your summary and decide whether it covers the important ideas in the paragraph. Next, decide how to shorten the summary to 15 words or less without leaving out any essential information. Write this summary below.

_____

_____

_____

_____

_____ Number of correct answers

Record your personal assessment of your work on the Critical Thinking Chart on page 104.

Critical Thinking

Follow the directions provided for questions 1, 2, and 5. Put an X next to the correct answer for the other questions.

1. For each statement below, write O if it expresses an opinion or write F if it expresses a fact.

_____ a. Burke and Wills began their journey on August 20, 1860.

_____ b. Robert Burke was not a great leader.

_____ c. Burke started his expedition with 20 tons of supplies.

2. Choose from the letters below to correctly complete the following statement. Write the letters on the lines.

On the positive side, _____, but on the negative side, _____.

a. Burke had no qualifications as an explorer

b. Burke was a forceful, determined man

c. Burke split up the group on the expedition

3. Of the following theme categories, which would this story fit into?

☐ a. Adventure Sports

☐ b. Fearless Explorers

☐ c. Problem Solvers

4. From what the article told about the men left waiting at the camp, you can conclude that they

☐ a. stayed longer than ordered because they were afraid they could not find their way back.

☐ b. lost track of the days, or else they would have followed orders and left after three months.

☐ c. waited longer than they had been told to because they hoped Burke and the other men were only delayed.

5. Which paragraph provides evidence that supports your answer to question 4?

_____

_____ Number of correct answers

Record your personal assessment of your work on the Critical Thinking Chart on page 104.

Personal Response

Would you recommend this article to other students? Explain.

_____

_____

_____

_____

Self-Assessment

I can't really understand how

_____

_____

_____

_____

_____

_____

_____

_____

_____

CRITICAL THINKING

James Herman Banning

Pioneer Pilot

Banning and Allen called their cross-country achievement "The Hallelujah Flight."

James Herman Banning fought a personal war on two fronts—one on the ground and the other in the air. As an African American born in Oklahoma in 1899, Banning faced racial prejudice in the form of laws that restricted his freedom in very many ways. His other war was fought in the skies as a black pioneer pilot. Flying a plane during the early days of aviation was risky business even for white pilots with plenty of financial backing, but it was even riskier for African American pilots. They often lacked the money to buy first-class equipment, and so they would wind up flying older planes patched together with hand-me-down parts. None of that, however, deterred Banning. He was determined, in the memorable words of poet and pilot John Magee, to slip "the surly bonds of Earth."

2   Banning was bitten by the flying bug when he was a young man. By then, his family had moved from Oklahoma to Ames, Iowa. Banning studied electrical engineering at Iowa State for a year and then set up the J. H. Banning Auto Repair Shop in Ames. He ran the garage from 1922 to 1928. During that time, flying became a national craze. Pilots such as Charles Lindbergh were popular heroes. Banning fell in love with the thought that he, too, would fly some day. Because he was an African American, however, one pilot school after another turned him down. Finally, his luck changed. A former U.S. Army pilot who ran a school in Des Moines accepted him. After Banning successfully finished his flying lessons, he became the first African American aviator in history to be licensed by the U. S. Department of Commerce.

3   In 1929 Banning left Iowa to live in Los Angeles and work as the chief pilot for the Bessie Coleman Aero Club. The club was named after a legendary pilot who was not only African American but also a female. No American flying school would take Bessie Coleman as a student, so she had gone to France to learn how to fly. Back in the United States, she performed as an aerial daredevil, trying to raise enough money to start her own flight school. Sadly, in 1926 she died when her controls locked, sending her plane crashing to the ground. The founder of the Bessie Coleman Aero Club was a visionary African American pilot named William Powell. He argued that the sky would open the door to freedom for his people. He did not want to look to white people for assistance. In his book *Black Wings*, Powell wrote that he aligned himself with the sort of young African American "who believes he has the brain, the ability, to carve out his own destiny."

4   Carving out his own destiny was exactly what James Banning had in mind. He set his sights on becoming the first African American pilot to fly across the country. By 1932 he and an African American mechanic named Thomas Allen set out in a two-seat biplane that was already six years old. Given the rapid development of aviation technology, this plane was almost ancient by the standards of the day. That, however, did not stop the two men. Banning and Allen rebuilt the old engine, fixed up the ignition system, and added valves from an abandoned Studebaker car found in a junkyard.

5   Flying east from Los Angeles, California, to Long Island, New York, they took off without even enough money for gas and oil. Skeptics called them the *Flying Hobos*, a thinly veiled jab at the pair's lack of resources. For the most part, they had good weather, although they did hit a couple of rough spots. They had to navigate through some difficult winds when going over the mountains, and they ran into

James Banning battled prejudice and unfair laws to make his dream come true.

patches of heavy fog. A bigger problem, though, was their finances. The two men solicited donations of food and supplies along the way. Even so, they sometimes had to choose between eating and refueling their plane. In New Mexico, Banning sold his watch and his spare suit to get money for gas. Friends and well-wishers often met them at stopovers and welcomed them into their homes. If there were no friends in sight, the two men slept in their plane or in old barns or abandoned railroad cars. Banning and Allen continued in this manner for the entire 3,300-mile journey. Despite the fact that they were in flight for only a total of 42 hours, it took them 21 days to reach Long Island's Valley Stream Airport in New York.

6   This cross-country achievement made James Banning famous. He suddenly was someone people would pay to see. Sadly, he did not live to enjoy this fame very long. On February 5, 1933, just three months after his historic flight, tragedy struck. It happened at an air show at Camp Kearney in San Diego, California. Banning was scheduled to fly an exhibition. His plan was to do some stunts and then fly to a height of 4,000 feet with a woman named Marion Daugherty, who would then make a parachute jump. Banning needed a plane to perform these feats, however, and that proved to be a problem. The local flight instructor did not trust a black man to fly a plane, so changes were made in the program. It was decided that a white Navy pilot named Albert Burghardt would fly the plane. Banning would come along as a passenger and would do the parachute jump himself.

7   With a crowd of over 2,000 watching, Burghardt took the plane into a steep climb. At 400 feet, however, the engine stalled. The plane went into a tailspin as Banning sat helplessly in his seat. Moments later, the plane crashed in front of the viewing stands. Rescuers lifted Banning from the wreck and rushed him to the hospital. With a fractured skull and internal injuries, Banning never regained consciousness and died about an hour later.

8   A newspaper account of the accident said that Banning had joined Bessie Coleman in the "Valhalla of Death." This was a sacred place, the article said, that was "reserved for those gallant souls who have the courage to face even death in an unequal struggle, with poor equipment and race prejudice." James Banning had challenged two powerful foes. He had pushed aside the restrictions that threatened to keep him earthbound. And, through his courage and determination, he had helped future African Americans find their own wings to fly. ✳

If you have been timed while reading this article, enter your reading time below. Then turn to the Words-per-Minute Table on page 101 and look up your reading speed (words per minute). Enter your reading speed on the graph on page 102.

Reading Time: Lesson 9

_____ : _____

Minutes   Seconds

A Finding the Main Idea

One statement below expresses the main idea of the article. One statement is too general, or too broad. The other statement explains only part of the article; it is too narrow. Label the statements using the following key:

M—Main Idea   **B—Too Broad**   **N—Too Narrow**

_____ 1. African Americans in the United States have had to overcome many challenges because of long-standing racial prejudice.

_____ 2. James Banning was turned away from several pilot schools simply because he was an African American.

_____ 3. James Banning successfully battled racial prejudice along with the dangers of flying with poor equipment to become a respected pilot.

_____ Score 15 points for a correct M answer.

_____ Score 5 points for each correct B or N answer.

_____ **Total Score**: Finding the Main Idea

B Recalling Facts

How well do you remember the facts in the article? Put an X in the box next to the answer that correctly completes each statement about the article.

1. Before James Banning became a pilot, he
   - ☐ a. ran an auto repair shop.
   - ☐ b. was a professor at Iowa State University.
   - ☐ c. worked with legendary pilot Bessie Coleman.

2. James Banning was the first African American to
   - ☐ a. fly a stunt plane.
   - ☐ b. join the Bessie Coleman Aero Club.
   - ☐ c. be licensed by the U. S. Department of Commerce.

3. Banning's cross-country flight took
   - ☐ a. 21 days.
   - ☐ b. 35 days.
   - ☐ c. 42 days.

4. The biggest problem on Banning's cross-country flight was
   - ☐ a. bad weather along the way.
   - ☐ b. lack of money for food and fuel.
   - ☐ c. that he had no experience in navigation.

5. James Banning died when the plane he was in
   - ☐ a. crashed on landing in San Diego, California.
   - ☐ b. hit the side of a mountain.
   - ☐ c. stalled in mid-air and then fell to the earth.

Score 5 points for each correct answer.

_____ **Total Score**: Recalling Facts

C Making Inferences

When you combine your own experiences and information from a text to draw a conclusion that is not directly stated in that text, you are making an inference. Below are five statements that may or may not be inferences based on information in the article. Label the statements using the following key:

C—Correct Inference   **F—Faulty Inference**

_____ 1. Many improvements were made to the engineering and construction of planes between 1926 and 1932.

_____ 2. To fly any plane in the United States during the 1920s, a pilot needed to be licensed by the U. S. Department of Commerce.

_____ 3. To James Banning, style and appearance were even more important than flying.

_____ 4. Often, people's career choices are influenced by what is currently popular.

_____ 5. The plane in which Banning died would not have stalled out if he had been flying it.

Score 5 points for each correct answer.

_____ **Total Score**: Making Inferences

D Using Words Precisely

Each numbered sentence below contains an underlined word or phrase from the article. Following the sentence are three definitions. One definition is closest to the meaning of the underlined word. One definition is opposite or nearly opposite. Label those two definitions using the following key. Do not label the remaining definition.

C—Closest   **O—Opposite or Nearly Opposite**

1. None of that, however, <u>deterred</u> Banning.

_____ a. encouraged Banning to action

_____ b. embarrassed Banning

_____ c. prevented Banning from acting

2. During that time, flying became a national <u>craze</u>.

_____ a. intense interest, fad

_____ b. celebration

_____ c. subject of no interest

3. <u>Skeptics</u> called them the *Flying Hobos*, a thinly veiled jab at the pair's lack of resources.

_____ a. reporters

_____ b. doubters

_____ c. believers

4. The two men <u>solicited</u> donations of food and supplies along the way.

_____ a. asked for

_____ b. refused

_____ c. needed

5. The founder of the Bessie Coleman Aero Club was a <u>visionary</u> African American pilot named William Powell.

_____ a. kind and generous

_____ b. one who has no imagination

_____ c. creative thinker

_____ Score 3 points for each correct C answer.

_____ Score 2 points for each correct O answer.

_____ **Total Score**: Using Words Precisely

Enter the four total scores in the spaces below, and add them together to find your Reading Comprehension Score. Then record your score on the graph on page 103.

Score	Question Type	Lesson 9
_____	Finding the Main Idea	
_____	Recalling Facts	
_____	Making Inferences	
_____	Using Words Precisely	
_____	**Reading Comprehension Score**	

Author's Approach

Put an X in the box next to the correct answer.

1. The main purpose of the first paragraph is to

☐ a. summarize the history of aviation during the 1920s.

☐ b. explain how James Banning became a pilot.

☐ c. present the challenges faced by James Banning.

2. How is the author's purpose for writing the article expressed in paragraph 8?

☐ a. This paragraph points out that both Bessie Coleman and Banning had died in plane crashes.

☐ b. This paragraph tells readers that Banning was an admirable man of courage and determination.

☐ c. This paragraph states that Banning's accident was the subject of a newspaper article after his death.

3. The author tells this story mainly by

☐ a. comparing different topics.

☐ b. describing events in the order they happened.

☐ c. using imagination and creativity.

4. What does the author mean by the statement "James Herman Banning fought a personal war on two fronts—one on the ground and the other in the air"?

☐ a. Banning battled both prejudice and the risks of flying.

☐ b. Banning tried to make a living and follow his dream.

☐ c. Banning was not afraid to make a few enemies to reach his goals.

_____ Number of correct answers

Record your personal assessment of your work on the Critical Thinking Chart on page 104.

CRITICAL THINKING

Summarizing and Paraphrasing

Put an X in the box next to the correct answer for question 1. Follow the directions provided for questions 2 and 3.

1. Choose the best one-sentence paraphrase for the following sentence from the article: "Banning was bitten by the flying bug when he was a young man."

   ☐ a. As a young man, Banning became very interested in flying.

   ☐ b. Banning was a young man when he first learned about flying.

   ☐ c. When Banning was a young man, a bug flew into him and bit him.

2. Complete the following one-sentence summary of the article using the lettered phrases from the phrase bank below. Write the letters on the lines.

Phrase Bank:

a. Banning's early life, education, and training

b. Banning's tragic death and a summary of his legacy

c. Banning's adventures as a pilot

The article "James Herman Banning" begins with

_____, goes on to describe _____, and ends with _____.

3. Look for the important ideas and events in paragraphs 4 and 5. Summarize those paragraphs in one or two sentences.

_____

_____

_____

_____

_____ Number of correct answers

Record your personal assessment of your work on the Critical Thinking Chart on page 104.

Critical Thinking

Follow the directions provided for questions 1, 2, and 5. Put an X next to the correct answer for the other questions.

1. For each statement below, write O if it expresses an opinion or write F if it expresses a fact.

   _____ a. James Banning was born in Oklahoma but moved to Iowa and then Los Angeles.

   _____ b. It is sad that James Banning did not live long enough to really enjoy his fame.

   _____ c. Pilots such as Charles Lindbergh were popular heroes during the 1920s.

2. Choose from the letters below to correctly complete the following statement. Write the letters on the lines.

In the article, _____ and _____ are alike because both were African American pilots during the 1920s.

   a. Thomas Allen

   b. James Banning

   c. Bessie Coleman

3. What was the cause of Bessie Coleman's death?

☐ a. The engine on her plane stalled.

☐ b. The controls on her plane locked up.

☐ c. She fell to her death from the wing of a stunt plane.

4. From what the article told about Thomas Allen, you can conclude that he

☐ a. was a good mechanic.

☐ b. knew how to fix only biplanes.

☐ c. didn't enjoy traveling with James Banning.

5. In which paragraph did you find your information or details to answer question 3?

_____

_____ Number of correct answers

Record your personal assessment of your work on the Critical Thinking Chart on page 104.

Personal Response

How do you think James Banning felt when the pilot schools refused to admit him?

_____

_____

_____

_____

Self-Assessment

I was confused about question _____ in section _____ because

_____

_____

_____

_____

_____

_____

_____

CRITICAL THINKING

Opposites Attract

Ruth Harkness knew she could capture a panda if she tried—and so she did.

R uth Harkness was probably the last person any of her society friends would have chosen to lead a great adventure. She was a chain-smoking, hard-drinking New York City socialite and fashion designer who wouldn't even walk a city block if she could take a taxi instead. Despite all of that, this party girl showed everyone, and maybe even herself, what could be done when a sense of purpose grows into an obsession.

2   Harkness's husband, William, was an avid hunter and an adventurer. In 1934 he informed his wife that on his next expedition he would try to capture a Chinese giant panda. This elusive species of bear was unknown to anyone outside of China, except for a small circle of zoologists. Giant pandas live in the remote and largely unpopulated bamboo forests along the Chinese-Tibetan border. A few stories had circulated about the existence of an animal that looked like a cross between a raccoon and a bear, but no panda had ever been captured, and no zoo in the world had ever housed one.

3   William Harkness had heard the stories, and he had made up his mind to capture a live giant panda and bring it back to the United States. He teamed up with his partner Floyd Tangier Smith, a professional animal collector, and the two of them left

for China in 1934. Two years later, in Shanghai, China, Bill Harkness still had not laid eyes on a giant panda. His search was cut short when he unexpectedly became ill and died from throat cancer.

4   William Harkness's death provided his 35-year-old widow with a small inheritance and a collection of expedition supplies stored in a room in Shanghai. Ruth Harkness felt she had inherited something else also—her husband's dream of being the first to capture a giant panda. When she told people that she wanted to finish her husband's work, few of them took her seriously. Women in the 1930s, especially high-society women, were not known for capturing wild animals. Harkness knew the odds were stacked against her. It was obvious she would need help. She tried to persuade her husband's partner to continue the expedition with her, but he would not even consider the idea. Meanwhile, her friends treated her plan as a great big joke.

5   None of this deterred Ruth Harkness. She set sail for Shanghai to arrange for her husband's burial and to make plans to continue his expedition. When she arrived in China, she made two decisions right away. First, she would leave behind her husband's arsenal of guns, since the mere thought of killing repulsed her. Second, she decided that capturing an adult giant panda was not practical; it would be far too scary to go after such a big creature. Besides, even if she managed to capture one, how would she transport it back to civilization? Harkness believed she could capture and

carry an infant panda, however. So instead of a gun, she packed a glass baby bottle and a few cans of baby formula. This plan seemed to her to make perfect sense.

6   After arriving in Shanghai, Harkness set out to find a Chinese guide she could trust. She found the right man in Quentin Young, a college student who also happened to be an experienced explorer. Together Harkness and Young mapped out a 1,500-mile journey into the highlands of China and Tibet. Young agreed to organize all of the details of the trip, including hiring the team of trackers, cooks, and porters.

7   The journey was brutal. Not only did the company endure temperatures as high as 100 degrees, but they also had to deal with local Chinese laws and restrictions, bandits, and other panda hunters. Harkness was much more used to bargaining with hotel doormen on Fifth Avenue, but she was a shrewd woman, and she was determined. She held the team together while also managing to keep a rigorous

Quentin Young (far right) organized and led Harkness's team into the mountains of China in search of the giant panda.

schedule that covered up to 30 miles a day on foot over rugged wilderness terrain.

8 In November 1936 the team arrived in the giant panda's natural habitat. They made their way through a dense grove of tall bamboo and waded through knee-deep moss that hid ponds of icy water. Within a few days, they met up with their prize. As she related in her book, "I stumbled blinded, brushing the water from my face and eyes. Then I stopped, frozen in my tracks. From the old dead tree came a baby's whimper." Young pulled the three-pound baby panda from the hollow of a rotting tree and handed it to Harkness. She was speechless. Harkness quickly formed a loving bond with the creature, which she named Su-Lin after Young's sister-in-law, who was also an explorer. The mission completed, the expedition turned around and headed for home. Ruth Harkness carried the nine-week-old Su-Lin in her arms and nursed it from the milk bottle she had brought.

9 Su-Lin's arrival in the United States caused an enormous sensation. The public had never seen a panda before, and they could not get enough. Photographers clamored for photos, and reporters showered Harkness with interview requests. People were fascinated by the adorable baby panda, but there was so much more to the story. In the middle of it all was this amazing woman—a novice explorer—who had captured him.

10 Harkness suddenly was famous, and her fame made her feel confident that she could re-create her journey. She wanted to bring back a companion for little Su-Lin, who was being cared for at the Chicago Brookfield Zoo. Harkness did return to China in 1937, and she and Young managed to capture a second baby panda, which she named Mei-Mei.

11 Su-Lin and Mei-Mei did not bond very well, however. The two pandas fought constantly and had to be separated permanently. A few weeks later, Su-Lin fell ill and died, and Harkness once again felt called upon to return to the bamboo forest. On this third adventure, she and Young found two more giant pandas, but these were not infants as the others had been. One was an adult male and the other a young female they named Su-Sen. The outcome was tragically different also. Harkness and Young may have had trouble controlling their panda captives. They were forced to shoot the adult panda, and Su-Sen was set free to return to her native habitat.

12 Harkness never again felt as vibrant and alive as she had when finding and caring for her baby pandas. In a few years, the media's interest faded, and so did her fame. On July 20, 1947, Harkness was found dead in a hotel room in Pittsburgh, Pennsylvania. Just 46 years old, she had died from the effects of alcoholism. Despite her tragic death, Ruth Harkness had helped people to appreciate the beauty and importance of wild animals and the need to protect their natural habitats. ✳

If you have been timed while reading this article, enter your reading time below. Then turn to the Words-per-Minute Table on page 101 and look up your reading speed (words per minute). Enter your reading speed on the graph on page 102.

Reading Time: Lesson 10

_____ : _____
  Minutes   Seconds

A Finding the Main Idea

One statement below expresses the main idea of the article. One statement is too general, or too broad. The other statement explains only part of the article; it is too narrow. Label the statements using the following key:

M—Main Idea   **B—Too Broad**   **N—Too Narrow**

_____ 1. Ruth Harkness was a New York socialite who traveled to China in 1936 and brought back the first giant panda to the United States.

_____ 2. In 1936 the giant panda was unknown to people outside of China.

_____ 3. Ruth Harkness, a prominent New York socialite, found a three-pound baby giant panda and named her Su-Lin.

_____ Score 15 points for a correct M answer.

_____ Score 5 points for each correct B or N answer.

_____ **Total Score**: Finding the Main Idea

B Recalling Facts

How well do you remember the facts in the article? Put an X in the box next to the answer that correctly completes each statement about the article.

1. William Harkness died in the city of
   - ☐ a. New York City, New York.
   - ☐ b. Shanghai, China.
   - ☐ c. Pittsburgh, Pennsylvania.

2. While carrying the first baby giant panda to the United States, Harkness fed it
   - ☐ a. bamboo shoots.
   - ☐ b. baby formula.
   - ☐ c. oranges and bananas.

3. The second baby giant panda Harkness found was called
   - ☐ a. Mei-Mei.
   - ☐ b. Su-Sen.
   - ☐ c. Su-Lin.

4. Ruth Harkness's giant pandas lived at the
   - ☐ a. Washington National Zoo.
   - ☐ b. Central Park Zoo in New York City.
   - ☐ c. Chicago Brookfield Zoo.

5. The number of giant pandas that Harkness brought to the United States was
   - ☐ a. two.
   - ☐ b. three.
   - ☐ c. four.

Score 5 points for each correct answer.

_____ **Total Score**: Recalling Facts

C Making Inferences

When you combine your own experiences and information from a text to draw a conclusion that is not directly stated in that text, you are making an inference. Below are five statements that may or may not be inferences based on information in the article. Label the statements using the following key:

C—Correct Inference   **F—Faulty Inference**

_____ 1. In the 1930s zoo keepers did not know very much about taking care of giant pandas.

_____ 2. William Harkness was one of the richest men in New York.

_____ 3. Harkness received funding and other help from the Chinese government on her expeditions.

_____ 4. Ruth Harkness enjoyed the attention she was given by the public.

_____ 5. Ruth Harkness was probably very upset by the death of the first panda she had brought back to the United States.

Score 5 points for each correct answer.

_____ **Total Score**: Making Inferences

D Using Words Precisely

Each numbered sentence below contains an underlined word or phrase from the article. Following the sentence are three definitions. One definition is closest to the meaning of the underlined word. One definition is opposite or nearly opposite. Label those two definitions using the following key. Do not label the remaining definition.

C—Closest   **O—Opposite or Nearly Opposite**

1. Ruth Harkness left behind her husband's guns because the thought of killing <u>repulsed</u> her.

_____ a. pleased

_____ b. disgusted

_____ c. scared

2. Ruth Harkness was a <u>shrewd</u> and determined woman.

_____ a. nasty, obnoxious

_____ b. sharp in practical matters; clever

_____ c. foolish, silly

3. The team managed to keep a <u>rigorous</u> schedule.

_____ a. troubling, bothersome

_____ b. easy-going, loose

_____ c. rigid, severe

4. In the middle of it all was this amazing woman—a <u>novice</u> explorer—who had captured him.

_____ a. beginning, inexperienced

_____ b. expert, professional

_____ c. famous, well-known

5. Ruth Harkness never again felt as <u>vibrant</u> and alive as she had when finding her baby pandas.

_____ a. dull, lifeless

_____ b. important, well-known

_____ c. energetic, full of life

_____ Score 3 points for each correct C answer.

_____ Score 2 points for each correct O answer.

_____ **Total Score**: Using Words Precisely

Enter the four total scores in the spaces below, and add them together to find your Reading Comprehension Score. Then record your score on the graph on page 103.

Score	Question Type	Lesson 10
_____	Finding the Main Idea	
_____	Recalling Facts	
_____	Making Inferences	
_____	Using Words Precisely	
_____	**Reading Comprehension Score**	

Author's Approach

Put an X in the box next to the correct answer.

1. Choose the statement below from the last paragraph that best describes the author's opinion of Harkness's legacy.

☐ a. "Harkness never again felt as vibrant and alive as she had when finding and caring for her baby pandas."

☐ b. "On July 20, 1947, Harkness was found dead in a hotel room in Pittsburgh, Pennsylvania."

☐ c. "Despite her tragic death, Ruth Harkness helped people to appreciate the beauty and importance of wild animals and the need to protect their natural habitats."

2. The author tells this story mainly by

☐ a. listing facts about giant pandas.

☐ b. recounting events in the life of Ruth Harkness.

☐ c. describing problems faced by female explorers.

3. What does the author imply by the statement "A few weeks later, Su-Lin fell ill and died, and Harkness once again felt called upon to return to the bamboo forest"?

☐ a. Zoo officials called Harkness and hired her to bring back another panda to replace the dead panda.

☐ b. Harkness felt so bad about the death of the panda that she needed to get away.

☐ c. Harkness felt responsible for replacing the panda that had died.

_____ Number of correct answers

Record your personal assessment of your work on the Critical Thinking Chart on page 104.

Summarizing and Paraphrasing

Put an X in the box next to the correct answer.

1. Choose the best one-sentence paraphrase for the following sentence from the article: "Harkness knew the odds were stacked against her."

   ☐ a. Harkness knew her chances of succeeding were not good.

   ☐ b. Harkness knew that people were placing bets against her.

   ☐ c. Harkness knew that her behavior was strange.

2. Read the statement from the article below. Then read the paraphrase of that statement. Choose the reason that best tells why the paraphrase does not say the same thing as the statement.

   Statement: Ruth Harkness was probably the last person any of her society friends would have chosen to lead a great adventure.

   Paraphrase: When Ruth Harkness's rich friends wanted an exciting experience, Ruth was the last person they would choose to lead them.

   ☐ a. Paraphrase says too much.

   ☐ b. Paraphrase doesn't say enough.

   ☐ c. Paraphrase doesn't agree with the statement.

3. Below are summaries of the article. Choose the summary that says all the most important things about the article but in the fewest words.

   ☐ a. After Ruth Harkness's husband died, Ruth followed his dream and brought the first giant panda from China to the United States.

   ☐ b. Socialite Ruth Harkness was the first to capture a giant panda, a baby she brought to the Chicago Zoo. She became famous briefly but later died of alcoholism.

   ☐ c. Ruth Harkness was a New York socialite who became famous for capturing and bringing back a baby panda. She named the panda Su-Lin.

   _____ Number of correct answers

   Record your personal assessment of your work on the Critical Thinking Chart on page 104.

Critical Thinking

Follow the directions provided for questions 1 and 3. Put an X in the box next to the correct answer for the other questions.

1. For each statement below, write O if it expresses an opinion or write F if it expresses a fact

   _____ a. Giant pandas should never be exhibited in zoos; they belong in the wild.

   _____ b. Ruth Harkness died at the age of 46.

   _____ c. Ruth Harkness was one of the greatest explorers of the 20th century.

2. From the article, you can predict that if Ruth Harkness were alive today, she would be

   ☐ a. leading hunting expeditions.

   ☐ b. promoting greater respect for wild animals.

   ☐ c. hosting her own talk show.

3. Choose from the letters below to correctly complete the following statement. Write the letters on the lines.

On the positive side, _____, but on the negative side, _____.

   a. Harkness introduced the American public to the giant panda

   b. Harkness sailed to Shanghai to arrange for her husband's burial

   c. Harkness and her partner were responsible for the shooting death of an adult panda

4. How is Ruth Harkness an example of the theme of *Trailblazers*?

☐ a. Harkness had been a fashion designer in New York.

☐ b. Harkness became famous for bringing back the first giant panda to the United States.

☐ c. While others had attempted to find a giant panda, Harkness actually showed the way to capture one.

5. From the information in paragraph 7, you can conclude that

☐ a. Ruth Harkness regretted going to China, but she did not want to give up her search.

☐ b. the Chinese government was disorganized.

☐ c. travel in the highlands of China was exceptionally difficult.

_____ Number of correct answers

Record your personal assessment of your work on the Critical Thinking Chart on page 104.

Personal Response

If I were the author, I would add

_____

_____

_____

_____

because

_____

_____

_____

_____

Self-Assessment

Before reading this article, I already knew

_____

_____

_____

_____

CRITICAL THINKING

Compare and Contrast

Think about the articles you have read in Unit Two. Choose three articles that describe a trailblazing journey or achievement in which you would have liked to have participated. Write the titles of the articles in the first column of the chart below. Use information you learned from the articles to fill in the empty boxes in the chart.

Title	What role would you have played?	What is one thing you would have done differently or better?	How would your participation have changed or improved the outcome?

Imagine that you were present during one of these explorations or adventures. Describe your feelings. _____

_____

_____

_____

Words-per-Minute Table

Unit Two

Directions If you were timed while reading an article, refer to the Reading Time you recorded in the box at the end of the article. Use this words-per-minute table to determine your reading speed for that article. Then plot your reading speed on the graph on page 102.

Lesson	6	7	8	9	10	
No. of Words	1138	1173	1221	1078	1139	
1:30	759	782	814	719	759	90
1:40	683	704	733	647	683	100
1:50	621	640	666	588	621	110
2:00	569	587	611	539	570	120
2:10	525	541	564	498	526	130
2:20	488	503	523	462	488	140
2:30	455	469	488	431	456	150
2:40	427	440	458	404	427	160
2:50	402	414	431	380	402	170
3:00	379	391	407	359	380	180
3:10	359	370	386	340	360	190
3:20	341	352	366	323	342	200
3:30	325	335	349	308	325	210
3:40	310	320	333	294	311	220
3:50	297	306	319	281	297	230
4:00	285	293	305	270	285	240
4:10	273	282	293	259	273	250
4:20	263	271	282	249	263	260
4:30	253	261	271	240	253	270
4:40	244	251	262	231	244	280
4:50	235	243	253	223	236	290
5:00	228	235	244	216	228	300
5:10	220	227	236	209	220	310
5:20	213	220	229	202	214	320
5:30	207	213	222	196	207	330
5:40	201	207	215	190	201	340
5:50	195	201	209	185	195	350
6:00	190	196	204	180	190	360
6:10	185	190	198	175	185	370
6:20	180	185	193	170	180	380
6:30	175	180	188	166	175	390
6:40	171	176	183	162	171	400
6:50	167	172	179	158	167	410
7:00	163	168	174	154	163	420
7:10	159	164	170	150	159	430
7:20	155	160	167	147	155	440
7:30	152	156	163	144	152	450
7:40	148	153	159	141	149	460
7:50	145	150	156	138	145	470
8:00	142	147	153	135	142	480

Minutes and Seconds

Seconds

Plotting Your Progress: Reading Speed

Unit Two

Directions If you were timed while reading an article, write your words-per-minute rate for that article in the box under the number of the lesson. Then plot your reading speed on the graph by putting a small X on the line directly above the number of the lesson, across from the number of words per minute you read. As you mark your speed for each lesson, graph your progress by drawing a line to connect the Xs.

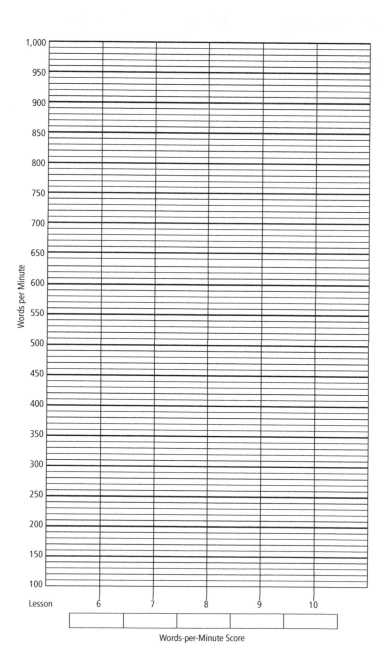

Words-per-Minute Score

Plotting Your Progress: Reading Comprehension

Unit Two

Directions Write your Reading Comprehension score for each lesson in the box under the number of the lesson. Then plot your score on the graph by putting a small X on the line directly above the number of the lesson and across from the score you earned. As you mark your score for each lesson, graph your progress by drawing a line to connect the Xs.

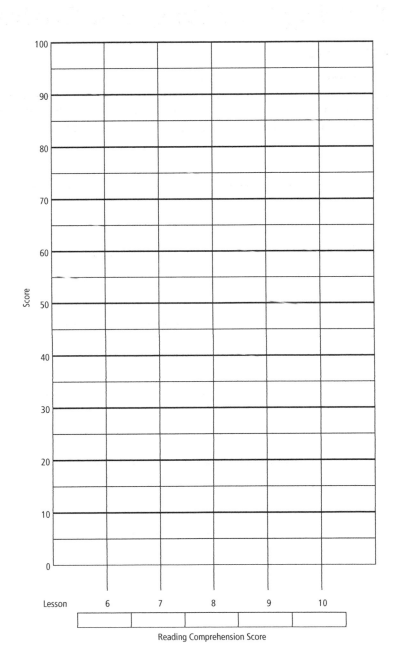

Reading Comprehension Score

Plotting Your Progress: Critical Thinking

Unit Two

Directions Work with your teacher to evaluate your responses to the Critical Thinking questions for each lesson. Then fill in the appropriate spaces in the chart below. For each lesson and each type of Critical Thinking question, do the following: Mark a minus sign (–) in the box to indicate areas in which you feel you could improve. Mark a plus sign (+) to indicate areas in which you feel you did well. Mark a minus-slash-plus sign (–/+) to indicate areas in which you had mixed success. Then write any comments you have about your performance, including ideas for improvement.

Lesson	Author's Approach	Summarizing and Paraphrasing	Critical Thinking
6			
7			
8			
9			
10			

Unit Three

The Wild Nile

Journey to the Source of the River

Explorers Neil McGrigor, left, and Cam McLeay paddle their inflatable motor boat after it broke down on the Nile near Cairo, Egypt.

The Nile is the world's longest and most mysterious river. It flows north for two-thirds the length of Africa and empties out into the Mediterranean Sea. But where does the river begin? In 2005 it was widely thought that the source was at Lake Victoria in southern Burundi. Three adventurers, Neil McGrigor, Garth MacIntyre, and Cam McLeay, thought they could prove that the Nile was fed by rivers extending beyond Lake Victoria, and that the true origin of the river was in the country of Rwanda. The men knew that a journey to the river's source would involve some danger. But they didn't fully understand the extent to which their ramble into the wilds of Africa would test their mettle.

2   Before these three men set out, no explorer had ever managed to travel all the way up the Nile. Every expedition had been stopped by impassable swamps, furious rapids, and plunging waterfalls. Other explorers had ultimately changed plans and took short-cuts overland from the east coast of Africa. Nonetheless, McGrigor, MacIntyre, and McLeay decided to conquer the river route by taking it all the way, trusting that technology would help them succeed where everyone else had failed. Their technology included a Global

Positioning System (GPS), motorized rafts, and a new invention called a "flying inflatable boat," or FIB for short. The FIB was like a motorized hang glider with a raft suspended from it that enabled the pilot to land on water as well as take off from there.

3   The British McGrigor and his New Zealand friends MacIntyre and McLeay departed from Alexandria, Egypt, on September 20, and at first they made good progress. The trio covered mile after mile, despite encountering a seemingly infinite number of snakes, lizards, and mosquitoes. Once they reached Uganda, however, the river grew narrow and they had to contend with new difficulties, including crocodiles, hippopotamuses, sharp rocks, and swirling rapids. Worst of all was the 140-foot Murchison Falls. The only way to get past these falls was to dismantle their motorized rafts and carry them piece-by-piece over the water using their flying inflatable boat. It took 16 trips in the FIB to get all the pieces safely above the falls.

4   Then the trip really got rough. On November 7, 2005, McGrigor flew ahead in the FIB, planning to meet the other men at an agreed-upon GPS location. By this time, a friend named George Heathcote had joined the expedition, so Heathcote, MacIntyre and McLeay launched their reassembled rafts and headed upstream through the churning rapids. But McLeay, an expert river rafter, incorrectly estimated the size of one massive section of rapids, and he flipped his boat end-over-end in the swirling, crocodile-infested water.

Heathcote and McIntyre helped get him to safety, but the raft was badly damaged.

5   Meanwhile, McGrigor was waiting upstream, wondering why his companions hadn't arrived at their rendezvous point. He flew the FIB downstream and looked for them. Flying low to get a better view, he accidently clipped a wing on a tree and crashed on the bank of the river. The FIB blew up on impact, and McGrigor, who suffered a broken leg, was badly burned in the crash. He crawled from the wreckage,

lucky to emerge with his life. The others heard the explosion and were surprised and relieved later when they found him alive.

6   Now, however, the group was stranded in the jungle and needed help. They were lucky that McLeay had a friend, Steve Willis, who owned a tourist lodge not too far away. McLeay called Willis and arranged to have him pick them up the next morning in his off-road vehicle. When Willis arrived, he brought an armed bodyguard with him, since this part of

The Tis Abay, or Blue Nile Falls, in Ethiopia was only one of many obstacles facing the exploration team.

Uganda was patrolled by an anti-government rebel group well-known for its violence and lawless behavior. As Willis drove the group toward the Murchison Falls National Park headquarters, they heard gunshots. "I looked in the rearview mirror and I could see one man in an olive uniform. I was looking down the barrel of his weapon," said McLeay. The group was being attacked by the rebel army.

7   The rebels shot out the truck's tires, and the vehicle veered off the road and into the tall grass. The explorers knew that if they stayed in the truck they would almost certainly be killed. The bodyguard jumped out of the truck and ran away with the group's only weapon. Steve Willis opened the driver side door and tried to run too, but he was hit by a bullet and killed instantly. McLeay made it through the rain of bullets and dived into the tall grass; Heathcote did the same. MacIntyre tried to scramble out of the truck, but as he did so, a bullet grazed his head. Although the wound was not serious, it caused him to bleed so profusely that the blood dripping into his eyes momentarily blinded him. Somehow, he managed to catch up with Heathcote, who guided him deeper into the tall grass.

8   The last one out of the truck was McGrigor, who couldn't run because of his broken leg. He crawled into the grass and hoped that the rebels wouldn't see him. They did, though, and they dragged him back to the truck, demanding his money and clothes. As McGrigor knelt on the ground waiting to be executed, the rebels stuffed dry grass into the truck and set it on fire. Then, for some unknown reason, they turned and fled, leaving McGrigor on the ground unharmed.

9   Hours later the surviving members of the group made it to safety. They were injured, shaken, and grieving for their dead friend. The men gave up the expedition and returned home. They decided to return to Africa the following year and continue their journey to find the source of the Nile. Neil McGrigor, Garth MacIntyre, and Cam McLeay wanted to finish what they had started, and they wanted to honor the sacrifice that Steve Willis had made in trying to help them.

10   And so on March 3, 2006, the explorers returned. Again, they fought their way up rapids, past hippos, and through swarms of mosquitoes. When the river ultimately became too shallow, they left their boats and traveled on foot until the river dwindled to a stream. At times, the men had to crawl to get through the thick jungle undergrowth. At last, however, they arrived at a muddy hole from where the first drops of the Nile water flow. The source was, as they had predicted, farther up into the highlands than anyone had realized, and it was indeed in the country of Rwanda. McGrigor, MacIntyre, and McLeay had proven that the Nile was 72.7 miles longer than anyone had previously known. ✶

If you have been timed while reading this article, enter your reading time below. Then turn to the Words-per-Minute Table on page 147 and look up your reading speed (words per minute). Enter your reading speed on the graph on page 148.

Reading Time: Lesson 11

_____ : _____
  Minutes   *Seconds*

A Finding the Main Idea

One statement below expresses the main idea of the article. One statement is too general, or too broad. The other statement explains only part of the article; it is too narrow. Label the statements using the following key:

M—Main Idea   **B—Too Broad**   **N—Too Narrow**

_____ 1. Determined to find the source of the Nile, three explorers faced danger and hardship before they achieved their goal.

_____ 2. For their 2005 expedition to find the source of the Nile, three brave explorers outfitted themselves with the latest technological devices, including a Global Positioning System, motorized rafts, and a flying inflatable boat.

_____ 3. Those who decide to explore the unknown often run into unexpected difficulties.

_____ Score 15 points for a correct M answer.

_____ Score 5 points for each correct B or N answer.

_____ **Total Score:** Finding the Main Idea

B Recalling Facts

How well do you remember the facts in the article? Put an X in the box next to the answer that correctly completes each statement about the article.

1. Until 2006 most people thought that the Nile began in
☐ a. Rwanda.
☐ b. Uganda.
☐ c. Burundi.

2. To get over the Muchison Falls required
☐ a. 16 trips in the FIB.
☐ b. two weeks of hard work.
☐ c. the help of a friend who ran a tourist lodge.

3. McLeay, an expert river rafter, had a problem when he
☐ a. flipped and damaged his raft.
☐ b. ran the FIB into a tree.
☐ c. broke his leg.

4. Rebel soldiers shot and killed
☐ a. Neil McGrigor.
☐ b. Steve Willis.
☐ c. George Heathcote.

5. The rebels quickly fled
☐ a. when they heard the sound of trucks approaching.
☐ b. for some unknown reason.
☐ c. when the bodyguard fired at them.

Score 5 points for each correct answer.

_____ **Total Score:** Recalling Facts

C Making Inferences

When you combine your own experiences and information from a text to draw a conclusion that is not directly stated in that text, you are making an inference. Below are five statements that may or may not be inferences based on information in the article. Label the statements using the following key:

C—Correct Inference   **F—Faulty Inference**

_____ 1. No cell phones work in the interior of Africa.

_____ 2. Spring and fall are both good times to set off on an exploration of the Nile.

_____ 3. The three explorers were competent mechanics, as well as adventurers.

_____ 4. Having an armed bodyguard with them probably saved the explorers' lives.

_____ 5. Steve Willis was aware of the dangers he was getting into when he agreed to help the explorers.

Score 5 points for each correct answer.

_____ **Total Score**: Making Inferences

D Using Words Precisely

Each numbered sentence below contains an underlined word or phrase from the article. Following the sentence are three definitions. One definition is closest to the meaning of the underlined word. One definition is opposite or nearly opposite. Label those two definitions using the following key. Do not label the remaining definition.

C—Closest   **O—Opposite or Nearly Opposite**

1. But they didn't fully understand the extent to which their ramble into the wilds of Africa would test their <u>mettle</u>.

   _____ a. cowardice

   _____ b. courage

   _____ c. patience

2. That is why some other explorers <u>ultimately</u> changed plans and took short-cuts overland from the east coast of Africa.

   _____ a. soon

   _____ b. finally

   _____ c. at first

3. The only way to get past these falls was to <u>dismantle</u> their motorized rafts and carry them piece-by-piece over the water using their flying inflatable boat.

   _____ a. take apart

   _____ b. build

   _____ c. steer

4. Meanwhile, McGrigor, waiting upstream, wondered why his companions hadn't arrived at their <u>rendezvous</u> point.

   _____ a. meeting

   _____ b. separating

   _____ c. special

5. Although the wound was not serious, it caused him to bleed so <u>profusely</u> that the blood dripping into his eyes momentarily blinded him.

_____ a. very little

_____ b. painfully

_____ c. in great abundance

_____ Score 3 points for each correct C answer.

_____ Score 2 points for each correct O answer.

_____ **Total Score:** Using Words Precisely

Enter the four total scores in the spaces below, and add them together to find your Reading Comprehension Score. Then record your score on the graph on page 149.

Score	Question Type	Lesson 11
_____	Finding the Main Idea	
_____	Recalling Facts	
_____	Making Inferences	
_____	Using Words Precisely	
_____	**Reading Comprehension Score**	

Author's Approach

Put an X in the box next to the correct answer.

1. The main purpose of the first paragraph is to

   ☐ a. inform readers of the goal of the expedition.

   ☐ b. compare old and new methods of exploring the Nile.

   ☐ c. encourage readers to learn more about the geography of Africa.

2. From the statements below, choose the one that you believe the author would agree with.

   ☐ a. The three explorers did not mind or even notice the discomforts of the journey up the Nile.

   ☐ b. The adventurers really appreciated the help that their friend Steve Willis gave them.

   ☐ c. The outcome of the expedition, that is, the discovery of the source of the Nile, was not worth the sacrifices.

3. Which of the following statements from the article best describes the way the adventurers felt just before they ended the 2005 expedition?

   ☐ a. "They were injured, shaken, and grieving for their dead friend."

   ☐ b. "The others heard the explosion and were surprised and relieved later when they found him alive."

   ☐ c. "But they didn't fully understand the extent to which their ramble into the wilds of Africa would test their mettle."

4. The author probably wrote this article to

☐ a. describe some of the technology used by modern explorers.

☐ b. inform the reader about the geography through which the Nile passes.

☐ c. express an opinion about explorers and the risks they will take to prove something.

_____ Number of correct answers

Record your personal assessment of your work on the Critical Thinking Chart on page 150.

Summarizing and Paraphrasing

Put an X in the box next to the correct answer.

1. Read the statement about the article below. Then read the paraphrase of that statement. Choose the reason that best tells why the paraphrase does not say the same thing as the statement.

Statement: Every previous expedition had been stopped by various problems, including impassable swamps, furious rapids, and plunging waterfalls.

Paraphrase: Although there had been previous expeditions, they had been abandoned when overwhelming difficulties arose along the way.

☐ a. Paraphrase says too much.

☐ b. Paraphrase doesn't say enough.

☐ c. Paraphrase doesn't agree with the statement.

2. Below are summaries of the article. Choose the summary that says all the most important things about the article but In the fewest words.

☐ a. To prove that the Nile began south of Lake Victoria, three adventurers followed the river all the way to its source in Rwanda. They relied upon modern devices such as GPS, motorized rafts, and a flying inflatable boat.

☐ b. In 2005 three adventurers, looking for the source of the Nile, were attacked by rebel soldiers in Africa. The soldiers killed one of their friends, but they escaped. They made it back to safety and abandoned their expedition until the next year.

☐ c. In 2005 three adventurers traveled up the river Nile to find its source. When one of their friends was killed by rebel soldiers, they stopped the expedition. They returned in 2006 and found the river's source in Rwanda, 72.7 miles past where others had thought it was.

_____ Number of correct answers

Record your personal assessment of your work on the Critical Thinking Chart on page 150.

Critical Thinking

Follow the directions provided for questions 1, 2, 3, and 5. Put an X in the box next to the correct answer for question 4.

1. For each statement below, write O if it expresses an opinion or write F if it expresses a fact.

_____ a. The adventurers proved that the Nile was 72.7 miles longer than it was thought to be.

_____ b. Crocodiles can be found in the Nile.

_____ c. The explorers should have known they would need more protection during the trip.

2. Choose from the letters below to correctly complete the following statement. Write the letters on the lines.

In the article, _____ and _____ are alike because they both come from the same country.

a. Neil McGrigor

b. Garth MacIntyre

c. Cam McLeay

3. Reread paragraph 7. Then choose from the letters below to correctly complete the following statement. Write the letters on the lines.

According to paragraph 7, _____ because _____.

a. MacIntyre was shot in the head

b. blood dripped into MacIntyre's eyes

c. MacIntyre tried to hide in tall grass

4. Of the following theme categories, which would this story fit into?

☐ a. Most worthwhile endeavors require effort.

☐ b. Friendship is more important than fame.

☐ c. Time heals all wounds.

5. In which paragraph did you find your information or details to answer question 2?

_____

_____ Number of correct answers

Record your personal assessment of your work on the Critical Thinking Chart on page 150.

Personal Response

This article makes me wonder why

_____

_____

_____

_____

Self-Assessment

While reading the article, I found it easiest to

_____

_____

_____

_____

_____

_____

_____

_____

CRITICAL THINKING

Being There

The Adventures of Benedict Allen

Benedict Allen led a five-and-a-half month expedition from Siberia through Mongolia.

He has been called "Britain's most fearless man," and few would disagree. Benedict Allen is a modern-day explorer and survivalist. In his relentless pursuit of adventure, Allen deliberately risks his life again and again in some of the most unwelcoming places in the world. Even more amazing, Allen does it without helpful technology such as a satellite phone or a Global Positioning System (GPS). This means that if Allen were to become disabled, detained, or injured in some isolated corner of the world, he would have no way of summoning help.

2   Allen took his first solo adventure in 1983 at the age of 22. He traveled by foot and dugout canoe from the mouth of the Orinoco River in northeast South America to the mouth of the Amazon River, a journey of 600 miles through one of the most remote forests on Earth. At one point gold miners attacked him, stealing all of his food, water, and possessions. Somehow Allen managed to drag himself out of the jungle despite being dehydrated and half-starved. He was also sick with dysentery and two types of malaria. Most people might have looked for a desk job in an air-conditioned office after that experience, yet all Allen could think about was planning for his next adventure.

3   In the early 1980s, Allen attempted many other journeys, including several that brought him close to death. He took a dog sled team across the frozen Arctic, almost perishing when he lost his dog team during a snowstorm. He endured a three-and-a-half month expedition with reluctant camels through the Namib Desert in southwestern Africa. He spent five months hiking in Mongolia, a journey that concluded in a six-week solo walk with camels across the length of the Gobi Desert. He spent nearly eight months crossing the widest point of the Amazon Basin, covering more than 3,600 miles. Allen was the first non-native to traverse the Central Range of Papua New Guinea. During his many adventures, he has been shipwrecked, shot at by drug dealers, and robbed by his trusted guides. Some people refer to him as a cat that has used up six of his nine lives.

4   Why does he do it? Allen himself admits that "I have never fully understood why I risk my life trekking though the Amazon, or walking across the Gobi. It may sound like a cliché, but I long to be out in the middle of nowhere, confronting nature." He expresses the feeling he gets after overcoming grueling adventures as

Explorer Benedict Allen is shown here at the edge of the Gobi Desert during his 1000-mile solo crossing.

"addictive." Allen is different from typical explorers who seek to be the first ever in history to see something or do something. To him, exploring is not about planting a flag as a conqueror, in fact, he says that his reasons are always exactly the opposite. He explains his passion for exploring as "making yourself vulnerable, opening yourself up to whatever's there and letting the place leave its mark on you." In other words, Allen travels not to reach the end but to experience getting there.

5   One place that literally left its mark on him is the Niowra village of Papua New Guinea. Allen went there when he was just 25 years old to witness a six-week male initiation ceremony. The ceremony, held to mark the passage of boys into adulthood, was called "Becoming a Man as Strong as a Crocodile." The old men in the village challenged Allen, telling him that he could be like other observers—missionaries and scientists—who sat on the sidelines taking notes, or he could learn what the Niowra culture was really about by actually participating in the ceremony. Allen couldn't resist, so he found himself, along with the other young men of the village, locked away in an arena and whipped every day for six weeks. The initiates were stabbed over and over with bits of sharp bamboo on their chests and backs. The resulting scars were meant to symbolize the ridges on the back of a crocodile. Allen

survived the six weeks and won the respect of the village elders.

6   These days, Allen's schedule usually calls for a one-year adventure followed by a year off to write a book about it. He also recently starred in travel shows for the British Broadcasting Company (BBC) as well as the History Channel. Before 2009 Allen had always traveled without a camera crew, using just his own hand-held camera to capture the essence of his adventure. But in 2009 he joined with a team from the History Channel to re-create the 1871 African expedition of Henry Morton Stanley, who searched for and found the missing explorer David Livingstone. The team included four explorers, two cameramen, and native porters. Except for the cameras, the team traveled the 970 miles exactly the way Stanley did, without any modern gear. They retraced Stanley's steps all the way to Tanzania, where Stanley found the missing Doctor Livingstone.

7   Allen's team almost died during this excursion. As Allen recalls, "We were crossing a river deep in the jungle, using flimsy dugout canoes just as Stanley had done 138 years before." Suddenly one of the porters panicked at the sight of crocodiles in the water, and he yelled and stood up in the canoe. The canoe started to wobble badly, and water leaked and splashed over the sides. Allen knew that if the canoe had

tipped over, "within a matter of seconds, the nesting crocodiles would have us all in their jaws," or to put it more bluntly, they would have been eaten alive. The team finally calmed down the frantic porter and steadied the canoe. Allen's team faced many other dangers also, and they were, he said, "always on the edge of trouble, with no way to summon help." When they finally reached the spot where Stanley met Livingstone, no one was surprised to hear Allen remark that "the struggles and hardships were worth it. . . ." In fact, the struggles and hardships actually may have been his favorite part of the trip. ✳

If you have been timed while reading this article, enter your reading time below. Then turn to the Words-per-Minute Table on page 147 and look up your reading speed (words per minute). Enter your reading speed on the graph on page 148.

Reading Time: Lesson 12

_____ : _____
Minutes   Seconds

A Finding the Main Idea

One statement below expresses the main idea of the article. One statement is too general, or too broad. The other statement explains only part of the article; it is too narrow. Label the statements using the following key:

M—Main Idea   **B—Too Broad**   **N—Too Narrow**

_____ 1. Benedict Allen travels around the world.

_____ 2. Author and filmmaker Benedict Allen risks his life exploring dangerous places without the help of modern inventions.

_____ 3. Benedict Allen's first adventure was in northeast South America when he was only 22 years old.

_____ Score 15 points for a correct M answer.

_____ Score 5 points for each correct B or N answer.

_____ **Total Score**: Finding the Main Idea

B Recalling Facts

How well do you remember the facts in the article? Put an X in the box next to the answer that correctly completes each statement about the article.

1. On his first solo adventure, Allen traveled in
    - ☐ a. southwestern Africa.
    - ☐ b. the Arctic.
    - ☐ c. South America.

2. Allen was the first non-native to travel across the
    - ☐ a. Namib Desert in southwestern Africa.
    - ☐ b. Central Range of Papua New Guinea.
    - ☐ c. widest point of the Amazon Basin.

3. Allen took part in an initiation ceremony in
    - ☐ a. the Gobi Desert.
    - ☐ b. Tanzania.
    - ☐ c. the Niowra village of Papua New Guinea.

4. When re-creating Henry Stanley's 1871 journey, Allen and the team from the History Channel traveled
    - ☐ a. 970 miles.
    - ☐ b. 600 miles.
    - ☐ c. 3,600 miles.

5. During that journey in Africa, Allen's team encountered
    - ☐ a. lions.
    - ☐ b. hippopotamuses.
    - ☐ c. crocodiles.

Score 5 points for each correct answer.

_____ **Total Score**: Recalling Facts

C Making Inferences

When you combine your own experiences and information from a text to draw a conclusion that is not directly stated in that text, you are making an inference. Below are five statements that may or may not be inferences based on information in the article. Label the statements using the following key:

C—Correct Inference   **F—Faulty Inference**

_____ 1. Allen travels without a satellite phone or GPS because he does not know how to use them.

_____ 2. The village elders made the initiation ceremony more difficult for Allen than for the other participants.

_____ 3. Allen does not plan his trips in advance.

_____ 4. Allen respects the customs of native peoples around the world.

_____ 5. Allen is a very independent man with many different skills.

Score 5 points for each correct answer.

_____ **Total Score**: Making Inferences

D Using Words Precisely

Each numbered sentence below contains an underlined word or phrase from the article. Following the sentence are three definitions. One definition is closest to the meaning of the underlined word. One definition is opposite or nearly opposite. Label those two definitions using the following key. Do not label the remaining definition.

C—Closest   **O—Opposite or Nearly Opposite**

1. Allen deliberately risks his life in his <u>relentless</u> pursuit of adventure.

   _____ a. never-ending

   _____ b. foolish

   _____ c. temporary

2. Allen longs to be out in the middle of nowhere, <u>confronting</u> nature.

   _____ a. appreciating

   _____ b. backing down from

   _____ c. facing or challenging

3. For Allen, overcoming <u>grueling</u> obstacles is habit forming.

   _____ a. constant

   _____ b. difficult

   _____ c. easy

4. On his adventures, Allen makes himself <u>vulnerable</u>, letting the place leave its mark on him.

   _____ a. distant

   _____ b. guarded

   _____ c. open to an experience

5. During the ceremony, the <u>initiates</u> were stabbed with bits of sharp bamboo.

_____ a. experienced members

_____ b. natives

_____ c. those being made part of a special group

_____ Score 3 points for each correct C answer.

_____ Score 2 points for each correct O answer.

_____ **Total Score**: Using Words Precisely

Enter the four total scores in the spaces below, and add them together to find your Reading Comprehension Score. Then record your score on the graph on page 149.

Score	Question Type	Lesson 12
_____	Finding the Main Idea	
_____	Recalling Facts	
_____	Making Inferences	
_____	Using Words Precisely	
_____	**Reading Comprehension Score**	

Author's Approach

Put an X in the box next to the correct answer.

1. The author uses the first sentence of the article to

☐ a. express an opinion about Britain.

☐ b. settle the argument about who is Britain's most fearless man.

☐ c. arouse the reader's curiosity about the person who is widely considered to be Britain's most fearless man.

2. Judging by statements from the article "Being There: The Adventures of Benedict Allen," you can conclude that the author wants the reader to think that

☐ a. Allen takes too many risks on his adventures.

☐ b. going on voyages without the help of modern inventions is reckless.

☐ c. Allen has chosen a life that is both demanding and exciting.

3. Which of the following statements from the article best describes Benedict Allen?

☐ a. "Allen took his first solo adventure in 1983 at the age of 22."

☐ b. "He has been called 'Britain's most fearless man,' and few would disagree."

☐ c. "Somehow Allen managed to drag himself out of the jungle despite being dehydrated and half-starved."

CRITICAL THINKING

4. From the statements below, choose the one that you think the author would agree with.

☐ a. Allen should not have tried to re-create Stanley's search for Dr. Livingstone.

☐ b. Allen planned to re-create the search for Dr. Livingstone because Allen wanted to honor Livingstone's memory.

☐ c. Allen re-created the journey Stanley took to find Dr. Livingstone because it would be an exiting adventure.

_____ Number of correct answers

Record your personal assessment of your work on the Critical Thinking Chart on page 150.

Summarizing and Paraphrasing

Put an X in the box next to the correct answer for questions 1 and 2. Follow the directions provided for question 3.

1. Read the statement about the article below. Then read the paraphrase of that statement. Choose the reason that best tells why the paraphrase does not say the same thing as the statement.

Statement: Allen survived the six weeks of the initiation ceremony, winning the respect of the village elders.

Paraphrase: Allen lived through the six weeks of the ceremony that left him with scars on his chest and back, and afterwards he was highly thought of by the older people in the village.

☐ a. Paraphrase says too much.

☐ b. Paraphrase doesn't say enough.

☐ c. Paraphrase doesn't agree with the statement.

2. Choose the sentence that correctly restates the following sentence from the article: "Allen took his first solo adventure in 1983 at the age of 22."

☐ a. In 1983 Allen planned to take his first unassisted adventure when he turned 22.

☐ b. In 1983, when he was 22 years old, Allen went on his first journey on his own.

☐ c. In 1983 Allen looked back at the first adventure he had taken when he was 22.

3. Look for the important ideas and events in paragraphs 6 and 7. Summarize those paragraphs in one or two sentences.

_____

_____

_____

_____

_____ Number of correct answers

Record your personal assessment of your work on the Critical Thinking Chart on page 150.

Critical Thinking

Follow the directions provided for question 1. Put an X in the box next to the correct answer for the other questions.

1. For each statement below, write O if it expresses an opinion or write F if it expresses a fact.

_____ a. Allen has starred in travel shows for the BBC as well as the History Channel.

_____ b. Benedict Allen is Britain's most fearless man.

_____ c. During his adventures, Allen has been shot at by drug dealers and robbed by his guides.

CRITICAL THINKING

2. Judging by Allen's willing participation in the six-week initiation ceremony as described in this article, you can predict that

☐ a. Allen would never again participate in a native ceremony for fear of being beaten and stabbed.

☐ b. Allen would recommend that tourists come and take part in the ceremony.

☐ c. Allen would join in another native ceremony if he were given the chance.

3. What was the cause of Allen's scars on his chest and back?

☐ a. being stabbed with sharp bits of bamboo

☐ b. being shot at by drug dealers

☐ c. being attacked by gold miners

4. How is "Being There: The Adventures of Benedict Allen" an example of the theme of *Trailblazers*?

☐ a. Allen makes films of his journeys to be shown on TV.

☐ b. Allen pursues adventures in the most remote areas of the world where few people have explored.

☐ c. Allen has almost died on some of his adventures.

5. From the information in paragraph 6, you can conclude that

☐ a. many people are fascinated by Allen's adventures and want to hear about them.

☐ b. Allen disliked traveling in Africa with inexperienced people.

☐ c. although Allen has used a camera on his trips, he isn't a very good photographer.

_____ Number of correct answers

Record your personal assessment of your work on the Critical Thinking Chart on page 150.

Personal Response

Why do you think Benedict Allen continued for the entire six weeks of the initiation ceremony?

_____

_____

_____

_____

Self-Assessment

I can't really understand how

_____

_____

_____

_____

_____

_____

_____

CRITICAL THINKING

The Unstoppable Cecilie Skog

Cecilie Skog is the first woman to have walked from the mainland of Europe to the North Pole.

People meet and fall in love in all sorts of places, but Cecilie Skog met her true love in a particularly unusual spot—on one of the highest mountains in the world. It didn't take long for Skog and Rolf Bae to find out they were perfectly matched. They were both young, attractive, and charismatic. They also were part of an elite new breed of "cross-over explorers" who excel not only at high-altitude climbing but also in the rugged world of polar exploration. Before long, Skog and Bae were trekking together to some of the most inhospitable places on Earth. They challenged each other, and they shared each victory and failure. But anyone who takes such risks will tell you: success and failure can be counted many ways, but tragedy is counted only once.

2   Cecilie Skog was born in Norway in 1974, and she developed an enduring love of the outdoors when she was a teenager. She trained to become a registered nurse, but starting at age 20, she spent much of her time climbing mountains. The more she climbed, the more she loved it, and eventually she felt skilled enough to climb the Seven Summits, which meant reaching the peak of the highest mountain on every continent. By 2004, when she started climbing with Bae, she had already completed North America, South America, and Europe. In that year, Skog went on to complete the final two climbs in Asia and Africa, but in addition to that, she and Bae decided to make treks to both the North and South Poles. Accomplishing these

journeys would make Skog the first woman to conquer the so-called Three Poles: the most northern point on Earth, the most southern point, and the highest point on Earth. Because she had already reached the summit of Mount Everest, she had only to reach the Poles to fulfill this goal.

3   Skog and Bae set out for the South Pole in November of 2005, accompanied by fellow adventurer Henry Borch. Wanting to make the journey the "real" way, they started from beyond Antarctica and made the entire journey without outside support. Despite having to endure temperatures that reached -70° F and taking a route that no one had ever used before, they arrived safely at the South Pole after just 33 days. As soon as they returned from this adventure, the threesome set out again, this time for the North Pole.

4   Most explorers consider the North Pole a more difficult target than the South Pole because the South Pole is on a continent, whereas the North Pole is a spot in the middle of the frozen Arctic Ocean. The Arctic ice shifts and drifts and often breaks up, causing explorers all kinds of navigational headaches. Skog, who pulled a sled full of supplies that weighed more than

twice as much as she did, found this expedition particularly difficult. At one point, Skog skied over a soft spot in the ice and fell through into the frigid water. After Bae and Borch helped her scramble out, they quickly put up their tent so she could climb inside and warm up, but the ice under the tent started to crack. Recalled Skog, "We had to literally get out and run as fast as we could, dragging the tent and our stuff 500 meters out of the way." After 48 days, they arrived at the Pole, and Skog became the 14th person and the first woman to conquer the Three Poles. A few days before they reached the North Pole, Bae bent down on one knee and proposed to her. The adventuresome couple were married on May 12, 2007.

Rolf Bae and Cecilie Skog had been married only a short time before the incident near the K2 summit.

5   It's a funny thing about extreme explorers: they always seem to find some new challenge to tackle. And so it was with Cecilie Skog. Having conquered the Seven Summits and the Three Poles, Skog turned her attention to K2, a notoriously dangerous mountain in Pakistan's Karakoram Range. Just a couple of hundred meters shorter than Mount Everest, the 28,351-foot K2 is the second-highest mountain in the world and is considered by many to be the most difficult mountain in the world to climb. Its weather is worse than Everest's, and its cliffs and crevasses require far greater technical skill. On Mount Everest, one climber dies for every ten who make it to the summit. On K2, the death rate is much higher, with one death for every four who reach the top. Skog and Bae had been on K2 in 2005 but had failed to reach the summit due to bad weather. So now, in the summer of 2008, they again climbed to the K2 base camp and waited, along with dozens of other climbers, for a break in the weather.

6   That break came on August 1 when, after weeks of stormy skies, the day dawned bright and clear. Climbing K2 involves finding a way through sections so narrow and treacherous that climbers must proceed single-file. Because some of the early climbers struggled in these tight passes, Bae and Skog had to wait for the others to make it through first. The delay caused them to be late in approaching the summit. The couple grew worried that they would not have enough time to reach the top and get back to base camp before dark. Bae was exhausted, and he decided to stop with fewer than 200 meters to go to the summit. He waited while Skog continued climbing with fellow Norwegian Lars Nessa. Skog and Nessa made it to the summit and very soon started back down, rejoining Bae just as the sun was setting.

7   A nighttime descent of K2 is never advisable, but the trio hoped that by using their headlamps they could descend safely to their camp 2,500 feet below the summit. The worst part would be getting past the Traverse, a 600-foot wall of ice with another huge ridge of ice overhanging it. Heading onto this wall, Bae took the lead, with Skog about 80 feet behind him and Nessa another 80 feet back. As Bae neared the middle of the Traverse, the mountain suddenly seemed to shudder. Skog heard a crack, then a roar, then the harsh, scraping sound of ice crashing down the mountainside. She looked for Bae's headlamp, but it had disappeared. *He* had disappeared, swept away in a deadly avalanche that had given them no warning. Shocked and distressed, Skog only made it back to camp with the help of Lars Nessa. She later learned that Rolf Bae was not the only one who had died on K2 that night. A total of 11 climbers had perished, making it the worst tragedy in the mountain's history.

8   In the wake of Bae's death, Skog swore off high-altitude climbing, saying that while she had once thought of K2 as a diamond, "now I hate it." She did return to polar exploration, first skiing across Greenland in 2009 and then across Antarctica in 2010. Speaking about these journeys, she told reporters that although she missed Bae intensely, her own dreams lived on. As she said, "I still dream about sleeping in tents, journeys, blowing wind, and moments that make me feel really alive." ✳

If you have been timed while reading this article, enter your reading time below. Then turn to the Words-per-Minute Table on page 147 and look up your reading speed (words per minute). Enter your reading speed on the graph on page 148.

Reading Time: **Lesson 13**

_____ : _____
Minutes   *Seconds*

A Finding the Main Idea

One statement below expresses the main idea of the article. One statement is too general, or too broad. The other statement explains only part of the article; it is too narrow. Label the statements using the following key:

M—Main Idea   **B—Too Broad**   **N—Too Narrow**

_____ 1. In a high-risk sport such as mountain climbing, danger is a constant companion.

_____ 2. Cecilie Skog successfully climbed the Seven Summits, the highest mountains on every continent.

_____ 3. High-altitude climber and explorer Cecilie Skog has achieved amazing success but has also had to endure the death of her husband and fellow climber, Rolf Bae.

_____ Score 15 points for a correct M answer.

_____ Score 5 points for each correct B or N answer.

_____ **Total Score**: Finding the Main Idea

B Recalling Facts

How well do you remember the facts in the article? Put an X in the box next to the answer that correctly completes each statement about the article.

1. Cecilie Skog was born in
   ☐ a. Tibet.
   ☐ b. Norway.
   ☐ c. California.

2. Before she took up climbing, Skog trained to become a
   ☐ a. nurse.
   ☐ b. lawyer.
   ☐ c. teacher.

3. The highest point on Earth is
   ☐ a. the North Pole.
   ☐ b. Mount Everest.
   ☐ c. K2.

4. Cecilie Skog was the first woman to
   ☐ a. climb K2.
   ☐ b. climb the Seven Summits.
   ☐ c. conquer the Three Poles.

5. Rolf Bae was killed
   ☐ a. when he fell into a hole in the ice on K2.
   ☐ b. by an avalanche on K2.
   ☐ c. in a fall from a cliff on K2.

Score 5 points for each correct answer.

_____ **Total Score**: Recalling Facts

C | Making Inferences

When you combine your own experience and information from a text to draw a conclusion that is not directly stated in that text, you are making an inference. Below are five statements that may or may not be inferences based on information in the article. Label the statements using the following key:

C—Correct Inference   **F—Faulty Inference**

_____ 1. Rolf Bae was disappointed that he could not reach the summit of K2.

_____ 2. Cecilie Skog is an unusually strong woman.

_____ 3. Daring explorers have set up challenges for each other around the world.

_____ 4. Skog and Bae did not let bad weather interrupt their climbs, even on dangerous mountains.

_____ 5. Skog and Bae were willing to take chances that most other people would not take.

Score 5 points for each correct answer.

_____ **Total Score**: Making Inferences

D | Using Words Precisely

Each numbered sentence below contains an underlined word or phrase from the article. Following the sentence are three definitions. One definition is closest to the meaning of the underlined word. One definition is opposite or nearly opposite. Label those two definitions using the following key. Do not label the remaining definition.

C—Closest   **O—Opposite or Nearly Opposite**

1. Both were young and <u>charismatic</u> and part of an elite new breed.

_____ a. athletic

_____ b. unappealing

_____ c. charming

2. These "cross-over explorers" <u>excel</u> not only at high-altitude climbing but also in the rugged world of polar exploration.

_____ a. do better than others

_____ b. underperform

_____ c. exist

3. Before long, Skog and Bae were trekking together to some of the most <u>inhospitable</u> places on Earth.

_____ a. untraveled

_____ b. harsh

_____ c. comfortable

4. Cecilie Skog was born in Norway in 1974, and she developed an <u>enduring</u> love of the outdoors when she was a teenager.

_____ a. lasting

_____ b. unusual

_____ c. short-lived

5. A nighttime descent of K2 is never <u>advisable</u>, but the trio hoped that by using their headlamps they could descend safely to their camp 2,500 feet below the summit.

_____ a. possible

_____ b. unwise

_____ c. sensible

_____ Score 3 points for each correct C answer.

_____ Score 2 points for each correct O answer.

_____ **Total Score**: Using Words Precisely

Enter the four total scores in the spaces below, and add them together to find your Reading Comprehension Score. Then record your score on the graph on page 149.

Score	Question Type	Lesson 13
_____	Finding the Main Idea	
_____	Recalling Facts	
_____	Making Inferences	
_____	Using Words Precisely	
_____	**Reading Comprehension Score**	

Author's Approach

Put an X in the box next to the correct answer.

1. The main purpose of the first paragraph is to

☐ a. introduce Skog and Bae and their story.

☐ b. explain why Skog enjoyed climbing and exploration.

☐ c. encourage readers to learn more about high-altitude climbing.

2. Choose the statement below that is the weakest argument for attempting to reach the Three Poles.

☐ a. It is challenging and exhausting.

☐ b. It encourages explorers to take unnecessary risks.

☐ c. Success gives explorers a sense of accomplishment.

3. The author probably wrote this article in order to

☐ a. inform readers that K2 is harder to climb than Mount Everest.

☐ b. persuade readers not to take up high-altitude climbing.

☐ c. tell an interesting story about courage and love.

4. What does the author mean by the statement "The Arctic ice shifts and drifts and often breaks up, causing explorers all kinds of navigational headaches"?

☐ a. Changing ice conditions make explorers feel ill.

☐ b. Explorers never know their exact location because the ice constantly changes.

☐ c. Changing ice conditions force explorers to constantly change their routes.

_____ Number of correct answers

Record your personal assessment of your work on the Critical Thinking Chart on page 150.

Summarizing and Paraphrasing

Follow the directions provided for questions 1 and 2.

1. Complete the following one-sentence summary of the article using the lettered phrases from the phrase bank below. Write the letters on the lines.

> **Phrase Bank:**
> a. Cecilie Skog's early accomplishments
> b. Cecilie Skog's most recent journeys
> c. what Cecilie Skog and Rolf Bae explored together

The article "The Unstoppable Cecilie Skog" begins with _____, goes on to describe _____, and ends with _____.

2. Below are summaries of the article. Choose the summary that says all the most important things about the article but in the fewest words.

☐ a. Cecilie Skog is an amazing mountain climber and explorer. Skog, along with her husband, went by foot to the South Pole and to the North Pole. Exploration is still one of her passions.

☐ b. When Cecilie Skog met Rolf Bae, she knew she had met her true love. Together they climbed some of the world's highest mountains. Bae died in 2008.

☐ c. Already a skilled climber, Cecilie Skog met and married climber Rolf Bae. Together they explored polar regions and climbed mountains until his 2008 death on K2. Skog continues to explore and to challenge herself.

> _____ Number of correct answers
> Record your personal assessment of your work on the Critical Thinking Chart on page 150.

Critical Thinking

Follow the directions provided for questions 1 and 5. Put an X next to the correct answer for the other questions.

1. Choose from the letters below to correctly complete the following statement. Write the letter on the lines.

On the positive side, _____, but on the negative side _____.

a. he died in a climbing accident

b. it took 33 days for Cecilie Skog and Rolf Bae to reach the South Pole

c. Cecilie Skog found a man with whom to share her life

2. What was the effect of the avalanche at the Traverse on K2 on August 1, 2008?

☐ a. Rolf Bae and 10 other climbers died.

☐ b. Cecilie Skog was finally able to reach the summit of K2.

☐ c. Cecilie Skog gave up exploring forever.

3. How is "The Unstoppable Cecilie Skog" related to the theme of *Trailblazers*?

☐ a. It shows that Cecilie Skog was a loving wife.

☐ b. It shows that Cecilie Skog chooses to live a life of adventure.

☐ c. It shows that Cecilie Skog never gives up in the face of adversity.

4. If you were a mountain climber or explorer, how could you best use the information in the article to stay safe?

☐ a. Always travel with one or more people.

☐ b. Accept only challenges that are at the extreme outer limits of your abilities.

☐ c. Never change your plans, even when conditions change.

CRITICAL THINKING

5. In which paragraph did you find your information or details to answer question 2?

_____

_____

_____ Number of correct answers

Record your personal assessment of your work on the Critical Thinking Chart on page 150.

Personal Response

What new question do you have about this topic?

_____

_____

_____

_____

_____

_____

_____

The part I found most difficult about the article was

_____

_____

_____

_____

_____

_____

I found this difficult because

_____

_____

_____

_____

_____

_____

CRITICAL THINKING

The Villas Bôas Brothers

Most of the Kayapó people still dress in the traditional style.

Orlando Villas Bôas just wasn't cut out for city life. He was born on January 12, 1914, and grew up on a coffee plantation about 150 miles northwest of the city of São Paulo, Brazil. He and his brothers, Cláudio and Leonardo, loved listening to their father's stories about adventures in Brazil's backcountry and his various encounters with native peoples there. When Orlando was 15 years old, his family moved to the Brazilian city of Rio de Janeiro. He worked as a desk clerk for years, but he was uncomfortable and restless in the big city. When he saw an opportunity for some real adventure, he leaped at the chance. So, too, did Cláudio and Leonardo.

2   In 1943 the three brothers signed up to join the Roncador-Xingu expedition, a government-sponsored project to explore and map the immense plains and jungles of Brazil's interior. At the time, the overwhelming majority of Brazilians lived along the eastern coastline, while the interior of the country was very sparsely populated. Brazil's president, Getulio Vargas, hoped to change that, so he adopted the national slogan, "March to the West." The goal of the Roncador-Xingu project was to prepare the way for new settlements in the wilderness by building roads, airstrips, and towns.

3   The brothers' attempts to join the expedition, however, did not begin very well. The head of the expedition didn't think they had the necessary survival skills for the project. To prove they were ready for the adventure, the brothers grew beards, put on grubby clothes, and tried to pass themselves off as manual laborers. They didn't remain laborers for long, however. When the head of the expedition found out they could read, Cláudio became chief of staff, Leonardo was put in charge of the warehouse, and Orlando found himself behind a desk again as a clerk.

4   The Roncador-Xingu expedition wasn't one of those quick-in-and-quick-out projects; it lasted nearly 20 years, coming to an end in 1960. Altogether, it opened up about 1,000 miles of new roads. It also mapped six previously unknown rivers, carved numerous landing strips in the jungle, and established contact with more than 100 indigenous nations. While these changes represented success to Brazil's leaders, they proved to be disastrous for the indigenous nations living there. These groups had formed their own societies for centuries without contact from the outside world. They had their own customs, economies, and values. But the Vargas government was determined to make Brazil's interior a model of modern life. As a result, the government showed no hesitation in clearing the forests that sustained these indigenous groups, removing the people or relocating them.

5   The Villas Bôas brothers became even bigger cogs in this government machine. They were often the ones who were sent to bargain with the local people to persuade them to let the expedition pass through their tribal lands. In 1948 Orlando, Cláudio, and Leonardo made contact with a number of groups, including the Xavantes, a fearless warrior society. These people were guided by the belief that hunting and eating certain animals produced dreams that allowed for communication with dead ancestors. The brothers also were the first outsiders to communicate with the Juruna, a people

Orlando Villas Bôas, one of Brazil's great explorers, is shown with his wife Marina, who was a 25-year-old nurse when she arrived to help on the reservation.

whose culture was strongly associated with the Xingu River, and also with the Kayabi, who believed that tattoos infuse people with special powers.

6   To advance the project and keep their jobs, the brothers allowed the indigenous tribes to be invaded and harassed. But the more time Orlando, Cláudio, and Leonardo spent in the jungle, the more they came to admire the strength and dignity of the people who lived there. They began to question the prejudices that many of the people they worked for held against the indigenous peoples. To communicate with the groups on a higher level, the brothers learned to speak several of the native languages. They came to understand that aggressive behavior sometimes shown by tribes toward outsiders could be justified, especially if the group felt their way of life might be threatened. The brothers learned that the local people had stable, organized societies in which no one went hungry and everyone lived well.

7   As their respect for the indigenous tribes increased, the Villas Bôas brothers vowed to protect them from the encroachment of civilization. They tried to prevent detrimental products such as alcohol from being imported into the villages. They also did their best to keep out visitors, tourists, and missionaries.

8   The brothers strongly believed that the unique cultures of the Xingu area had to be protected from outside influences. They believed the best way to do this was to give the groups an area that was theirs alone—a place with boundaries that would be respected by outsiders. In 1961 the brothers joined with other professionals to create the Xingu National Park. This park, which today covers about 12,000 square miles, was planned as a safe haven, where tribes could live together relatively undisturbed by the outside world. Moving to the park was not an easy decision, and some groups resisted. But the brothers knew they could not stop the continuing upheaval of Indian ancestral lands. They believed that the park would help the tribes to preserve at least some of their traditions and native culture.

9   Leonardo Villas Bôas died in 1961, but Cláudio and Orlando carried on their work for another two decades. The two brothers lived in the Xingu Indian reservation and fought to keep outsiders from interfering with the 17 tribal groups that moved there. Cláudio and Orlando established a health clinic to treat the Indians against diseases carried by white outsiders. The brothers also encouraged the tribes to run their individual governments in their own way and maintain as much of their culture as possible. For their efforts, the brothers became legendary around the world among environmentalists and human rights activists. Brazilian anthropologist Carmen Junqueira praised them by saying, "The Roncador-Xingu expedition opened up a space for our society to advance: luckily for the Indians, Orlando and his brothers were on it. If it hadn't been for their presence, maybe there wouldn't be any more Indians in the region."

10   Cláudio Villas Bôas died in 1998, and the people of the Xingu held a special ceremony in his honor. When the 84-year-old Orlando arrived on the scene, he was embraced by every elderly man and woman present. The rituals performed that night under the light of the moon capture the essence of what the Villas Bôas brothers meant to the people of the Xingu. A painted pole representing Cláudio was erected in the center of the village. This was a token befitting a great chief. Then, as one observer described it, "A small fire burned in front of this pole and pairs of shamans chanted quietly and melodiously in honor of their departed champion." ✴

If you have been timed while reading this article, enter your reading time below. Then turn to the Words-per-Minute Table on page 147 and look up your reading speed (words per minute). Enter your reading speed on the graph on page 148.

Reading Time: Lesson 14

_____ : _____
Minutes   Seconds

A Finding the Main Idea

One statement below expresses the main idea of the article. One statement is too general, or too broad. The other statement explains only part of the article; it is too narrow. Label the statements using the following key:

M—Main Idea   **B—Too Broad**   **N—Too Narrow**

_____ 1. In 1943 the Villas Bôas brothers joined the Roncador-Xingu project.

_____ 2. The cultures of some indigenous peoples in Brazil have been threatened by modern civilization.

_____ 3. The Villas Bôas brothers spent much of their lives protecting the indigenous peoples of Brazil.

_____ Score 15 points for a correct M answer.

_____ Score 5 points for each correct B or N answer.

_____ **Total Score**: Finding the Main Idea

B Recalling Facts

How well do you remember the facts in the article? Put an X in the box next to the answer that correctly completes each statement about the article.

1. When Orlando was 15 years old, his family moved to
   ☐ a. São Paulo, Brazil.
   ☐ b. Rio do Janeiro, Brazil.
   ☐ c. a coffee plantation.

2. In 1943 the Brazilian president adopted the slogan
   ☐ a. "New Settlements Now."
   ☐ b. "Prepare the Way."
   ☐ c. "March to the West."

3. The Kayabi people believed that
   ☐ a. tattoos gave people special powers.
   ☐ b. eating certain animals produced dreams.
   ☐ c. they could communicate with the dead in their dreams.

4. The Roncador-Xingu expedition established contact with more than
   ☐ a. 100 tribal groups.
   ☐ b. 17 tribal groups.
   ☐ c. 20 tribal groups.

5. Today the Xingu National Park covers about
   ☐ a. 150 square miles.
   ☐ b. 1,000 square miles.
   ☐ c. 12,000 square miles.

Score 5 points for each correct answer.

_____ **Total Score**: Recalling Facts

C Making Inferences

When you combine your own experiences and information from a text to draw a conclusion that is not directly stated in that text, you are making an inference. Below are five statements that may or may not be inferences based on information in the article. Label the statements using the following key:

C—Correct Inference   **F—Faulty Inference**

_____ 1. The Indian tribes of Brazil have very little interaction with the rest of the country's population.

_____ 2. In the 1940s, travel in the interior of Brazil was difficult.

_____ 3. The Brazilian Indians lead simple, uncomplicated lives.

_____ 4. The Villas Bôas brothers were the only members of the Roncador-Xingu expedition that respected indigenous people.

_____ 5. The indigenous people of the Xingu National Park prefer living there to where they had been living.

Score 5 points for each correct answer.

_____ **Total Score**: Making Inferences

D Using Words Precisely

Each numbered sentence below contains an underlined word or phrase from the article. Following the sentence are three definitions. One definition is closest to the meaning of the underlined word. One definition is opposite or nearly opposite. Label those two definitions using the following key. Do not label the remaining definition.

C—Closest   **O—Opposite or Nearly Opposite**

1. The Kayabi believed tattoos underlined infused people with special powers.

   _____ a. brought together

   _____ b. emptied

   _____ c. filled up, saturated

2. At first, the brothers allowed the indigenous tribes to be invaded and harassed.

   _____ a. tormented, hassled

   _____ b. assisted, supported

   _____ c. bargained with

3. The Villas Bôas brothers vowed to protect the indigenous tribes from the encroachment of civilization.

   _____ a. withdrawal

   _____ b. confusion

   _____ c. invasion

4. The brothers tried to prevent detrimental products such as alcohol from being imported into native villages.

   _____ a. harmful

   _____ b. modern

   _____ c. useful

5. The Villas Bôas brothers knew they could not stop the continuing <u>upheaval</u> of Indian ancestral lands.

_____ a. sudden, violent change

_____ b. staying the same; inactivity

_____ c. unlawful use

_____ Score 3 points for each correct C answer.

_____ Score 2 points for each correct O answer.

_____ **Total Score**: Using Words Precisely

Enter the four total scores in the spaces below, and add them together to find your Reading Comprehension Score. Then record your score on the graph on page 149.

Score	Question Type	Lesson 14
_____	Finding the Main Idea	
_____	Recalling Facts	
_____	Making Inferences	
_____	Using Words Precisely	
_____	**Reading Comprehension Score**	

Author's Approach

Put an X in the box next to the correct answer.

1. What is the author's purpose in writing this article?

☐ a. to introduce the reader to the important human rights activities of the Villas Bôas brothers

☐ b. to inform the reader about the Roncador-Xingu expedition

☐ c. to teach the reader some of Brazil's history

2. From the statements below, choose the two that you believe the author would agree with.

☐ a. The Villas Bôas brothers were cruel in encouraging the native tribes to move to the Xingu National Park.

☐ b. The work of the Villas Bôas brothers is admirable and worthy of our respect.

☐ c. The Villas Bôas brothers devoted much of their lives to the defense of the Brazilian Indian peoples.

3. What does the author imply by saying "They also did their best to keep out visitors, tourists, and missionaries" from the native villages?

☐ a. The brothers did not want visitors, tourists, or missionaries to influence the natives and bring about a change in their culture.

☐ b. The brothers did not want anyone—even visitors, tourists, and missionaries—to see what they were doing.

☐ c. The brothers were afraid the natives would attack the visitors, tourists, and missionaries because they were strangers.

_____ Number of correct answers

Record your personal assessment of your work on the Critical Thinking Chart on page 150.

CRITICAL THINKING

Summarizing and Paraphrasing

Put an X in the box next to the correct answer for question 1. Follow the directions provided for questions 2 and 3.

1. Choose the best one-sentence paraphrase for the following sentence from the article: "Orlando Villas Bôas just wasn't cut out for city life."

   ☐ a. Orlando Villas Bôas was afraid of the city.

   ☐ b. Orlando Villas Bôas did not enjoy city life.

   ☐ c. Orlando Villas Bôas had never lived in a city.

2. Complete the following one-sentence summary of the article using the lettered phrases from the phrase bank below. Write the letters on the lines.

   Phrase Bank:

   a. a description of the early life of the Villas Bôas brothers

   b. the ceremony in honor of Cláudio Villas Bôas

   c. the lifelong work of the Villas Bôas brothers

   The article, "The Villas Bôas Brothers" begins with _____, goes on to describe _____, and ends with _____.

3. Reread paragraph 8 in the article. Below, write a summary of the paragraph in no more than 25 words.

   _____

   _____

   _____

   _____

   _____

   _____

Reread your summary and decide whether it covers the important ideas in the paragraph. Next, decide how to shorten the summary to 15 words or less without leaving out any essential information. Write this summary below.

_____

_____

_____

_____ Number of correct answers

Record your personal assessment of your work on the Critical Thinking Chart on page 150.

Critical Thinking

Put an X next to the correct answer for questions 1, 3, 4, and 5. Follow the directions provided for question 2.

1. Which of the following statements from the article is an opinion rather than a fact?

   ☐ a. The brothers joined with other professionals to create the Xingu National Park in 1961.

   ☐ b. The native tribes had their own customs, economies, and values.

   ☐ c. Luckily for the Indians, Orlando and his brothers were on the Roncador-Xingu expedition.

2. Choose from the letters below to correctly complete the following statement. Write the letters on the lines.

   On the positive side, _____, but on the negative side, _____.

   a. many native tribes can no longer live in their ancestral lands

   b. many native tribes live undisturbed in the Xingu National Park

   c. many native tribes have their own languages

3. Of the following theme categories, which would this story fit into?
- ☐ a. Human Rights Activists
- ☐ b. Indian Cultures
- ☐ c. Travel in South America

4. Judging by events in the article, you can conclude that
- ☐ a. the Roncador-Xingu expedition was a total failure.
- ☐ b. Brazilians now show more respect for Indian cultures than they did in the 1940s.
- ☐ c. Brazilians now show less respect for Indian cultures than they did in the 1940s.

5. What did you have to do to answer question 2?
- ☐ a. find a comparison (how things are the same)
- ☐ b. find a contrast (how things are different)
- ☐ c. draw a conclusion (a sensible statement based on the text and your experience)

_____ Number of correct answers

Record your personal assessment of your work on the Critical Thinking Chart on page 150.

Personal Response

How do you think you would feel if the government forced you and your family to leave your home?

_____

_____

_____

_____

Self-Assessment

I was confused about question _____ in section _____ because

_____

_____

_____

_____

_____

_____

_____

_____

CRITICAL THINKING

The Badwater Ultramarathon

Lisa Tamati was the first over the finish line at the 2009 Badwater Ultramarathon.

There were moments, Lisa Tamati says, when she just wanted to lie down and die. Her body was exhausted, and her mind kept slipping into hallucinations. Alternating between nausea and fainting spells, she struggled just to keep her eyes open. She says. "There were times when I was sleepwalking, almost standing directly on a sleeping rattlesnake, vomiting, passing out, and collapsing on the road. . . ." Welcome to the Badwater Ultramarathon, the most brutal ultramarathon in the world. Given Tamati's description of her 2009 experience, it is no wonder some people refer to the race as "Satan's Fun Run."

2   Standard marathons such as the famed Boston Marathon or the New York City Marathon are 26.2 miles long. That's hardly a warm-up for the rare breed of runners who participate in ultramarathons. Although the definition of an ultramarathon is any foot race longer than 26.2 miles, the three most typical distances are 50 miles, 100 kilometers (about 62 miles), and 100 miles. Anything longer is usually defined by the time period allotted for completion. In the Badwater Ultramarathon, for instance, you have

60 hours to complete the course. And just how long is the Badwater race? This challenging competition is an astonishing 135 miles long. It starts 280 feet below sea level in Death Valley, California, the lowest point in the Western Hemisphere, and ends at 8,360 feet above sea level, halfway up California's Mount Whitney. The route takes runners up and down three mountain ranges as well as through the brutal heat of the Mojave Desert, where temperatures rise to 135°F.

3   City marathons such as those in Boston and New York attract tens of thousands of runners every year, though only a handful has a legitimate chance to win. Most of the runners are simply enthusiastic joggers out to test themselves. The Badwater Ultramarathon, however, does not admit amateurs. It is an invitational race, with only 80 to 90 runners allowed to run in any given year. To get accepted into the race, runners face stiff competition from an international talent pool. The organizers are extremely strict about who gets to run and who doesn't. For safety reasons if nothing else, they limit the field to only the most experienced extreme-distance runners.

4   To apply for the Badwater race, you have to meet one of the following Minimum Qualifying Standards:

1. You must have officially finished the Badwater Ultramarathon before *and* you must have completed at least one extreme running event within the past 12 months.

2. You must have officially finished at least three running races of at least 100 continuous miles, at least one of them in the previous 12 months.

Meeting these standards does not guarantee you will be accepted into the race; it merely allows you to apply. A committee then reviews your application and decides whether or not you make the cut. If you do make it in, you have to pay close to $1000 in fees for the privilege of experiencing what many call "hell on earth."

5   Despite the superhuman demands of the Badwater Marathon, it attracts adventure racers from around the world. In addition to bragging rights, racers who complete the course in fewer than 48 hours receive the coveted Badwater silver belt

Zach Gingerich's crew cools him off as he runs through Death Valley, California, on the way to winning the Badwater Ultramarathon 2010.

buckle. That's right—no six-figure check, no lucrative job offers—just a belt buckle. As race veteran Marshall Ulrich says, however, "To talk about the buckle is to miss the point." Ulrich has finished the race more than a dozen times. He was 28 years old when his doctor warned him to get off the couch and start exercising to lower his high blood pressure. Still running in his late 50s, Ulrich says that ultramarathoning has helped him find personal freedom and get in touch with his essential values. "There's something in you that wants to get out there in the middle of nowhere," he says. Ulrich adds, "We are built to run, to cover great distance, for survival's sake."

6   Like Marshall Ulrich, many participants in the Badwater Ultramarathon have private reasons for subjecting themselves to this brutal test of endurance. At least one runner, however, has used the race for a public cause. Martin Franklin, chief executive officer for a major corporation, used his 2010 run to raise money for the Wounded Warrior Project. This organization helps severely injured veterans from the wars in Iraq and Afghanistan to get training and jobs they need when they return home. Franklin got businesses to contribute money for each mile he ran, and he himself donated $135,000, or $1,000 per mile. When asked why he was raising money, Martin said, "Because, in a small way, this grueling run symbolizes the challenges our military veterans face when coming home from active duty."

7   *Grueling* really is the operative word. The desert heat of the Badwater Ultramarathon is notorious for causing dehydration, which can easily lead to organ failure and brain damage. There is the danger of not getting the proper amount of salt, which can cause people's hands and feet to swell like a balloon. There is also the risk of heat stroke. In a race this long, runners must contend with lack of sleep as well as dozens of painful blisters on their feet. Blisters may sound like the least of a marathoner's worries, but if not treated immediately, a tiny blister can explode into a crippling wound. Badwater runners also have to watch their step, since running straight through the night makes it hard to see where they are going, and they could easily twist an ankle or—as Lisa Tamati discovered—step on a rattlesnake.

8   Because so few racers cover such a vast distance, each one must have a support crew. Crew members ride in vans alongside the runner to monitor the runner's health and provide whatever food and drink he or she needs. The support crew carries buckets of ice to cool the runner down. Crew members also carry an assortment of bandages and ointments. Some even carry a variety of different-sized running shoes, since the runners' feet tend to swell as the race drags on. Finally, support crews contain pacers, people who take turns running with the racers and offering them encouragement. "My fate was within the hands of my amazing crew who talked me through every step," says Tamati. "Without

them I would not have been able to push through the pain to complete the race." Tamati did finish, and since her time was 37 hours and 14 minutes, she walked away with her very own Badwater belt buckle.

9   Although the Badwater Ultramarathon is not for everyone, those who have conquered it say they will never forget the triumph of crossing the finish line. Badwater racer Dr. Lisa Bliss, who is also the head of the medical staff for the race, understands both its allure and its dangers. Dr. Bliss is candid when she says, "No one can say that running 135 miles in the desert is healthy." But, she adds, "I'm not going to say it isn't one of the most incredible experiences of your life." ✳

If you have been timed while reading this article, enter your reading time below. Then turn to the Words-per-Minute Table on page 147 and look up your reading speed (words per minute). Enter your reading speed on the graph on page 148.

Reading Time: Lesson 15

_____ : _____
Minutes   Seconds

A Finding the Main Idea

One statement below expresses the main idea of the article. One statement is too general, or too broad. The other statement explains only part of the article; it is too narrow. Label the statements using the following key:

M—Main Idea   **B—Too Broad**   **N—Too Narrow**

_____ 1. The Badwater Ultramarathon is a difficult, invitation-only, 135 mile race that starts in Death Valley and ends halfway up Mount Whitney.

_____ 2. The Badwater Ultramarathon is a race that takes place in southern California.

_____ 3. The Badwater Ultramarathon is a race that awards a belt buckle to those contestants who finish in fewer than 48 hours.

_____ Score 15 points for a correct M answer.

_____ Score 5 points for each correct B or N answer.

_____ **Total Score:** Finding the Main Idea

B Recalling Facts

How well do you remember the facts in the article? Put an X in the box next to the answer that correctly completes each statement about the article.

1. The length of a standard marathon is
    ☐ a. 50 miles.
    ☐ b. 26.2 miles.
    ☐ c. 100 kilometers.

2. The length of time that runners in the Badwater Ultramarathon are given to complete the course is
    ☐ a. 48 hours.
    ☐ b. 60 hours.
    ☐ c. 2 days.

3. The lowest point in the Western Hemisphere is
    ☐ a. 8,360 feet below sea level.
    ☐ b. 135 feet below sea level.
    ☐ c. 280 feet below sea level.

4. The Wounded Warrior Project is
    ☐ a. a club of runners who have completed the Badwater Ultamarathon.
    ☐ b. a club of runners who have attempted but could not complete the Badwater Ultramarathon.
    ☐ c. an organization that helps injured veterans.

5. Not getting the proper amount of salt can cause
    ☐ a. organ failure.
    ☐ b. swollen hands and feet.
    ☐ c. heat stroke.

Score 5 points for each correct answer.

_____ **Total Score:** Recalling Facts

C Making Inferences

When you combine your own experiences and information from a text to draw a conclusion that is not directly stated in that text, you are making an inference. Below are five statements that may or may not be inferences based on information in the article. Label the statements using the following key:

C—Correct Inference   **F—Faulty Inference**

_____ 1. The Badwater Ultramarathon is considered a long race, even compared to other ultramarathons.

_____ 2. The race's organizing committee receives thousands of applications.

_____ 3. Many of the runners in the Badwater Ultramarathon suffer an injury during the race.

_____ 4. Not all of the runners are able to complete the Badwater Ultramarathon.

_____ 5. Runners who participate in standard marathons never run in ultramarathons.

Score 5 points for each correct answer.

_____ **Total Score**: Making Inferences

D Using Words Precisely

Each numbered sentence below contains an underlined word or phrase from the article. Following the sentence are three definitions. One definition is closest to the meaning of the underlined word. One definition is opposite or nearly opposite. Label those two definitions using the following key. Do not label the remaining definition.

C—Closest   **O—Opposite or Nearly Opposite**

1. Only a handful of runners have a legitimate chance to win a major city marathon.

_____ a. unrealistic

_____ b. reasonable

_____ c. fantastic

2. Some racers receive the coveted Badwater silver belt buckle.

_____ a. not wanted

_____ b. valuable

_____ c. greatly desired

3. Those who finish the race receive no lucrative job offers.

_____ a. money-making

_____ b. unprofitable

_____ c. possible

4. Dr. Bliss understands both the allure and dangers of the race.

_____ a. appeal

_____ b. risks

_____ c. repulsion

5. The head of the medical staff is <u>candid</u> when she says, "No one can say that running in the desert is healthy."

_____ a. discouraging

_____ b. lying

_____ c. telling it like it is

_____ Score 3 points for each correct C answer.

_____ Score 2 points for each correct O answer.

_____ **Total Score**: Using Words Precisely

Enter the four total scores in the spaces below, and add them together to find your Reading Comprehension Score. Then record your score on the graph on page 149.

Score	Question Type	Lesson 15
_____	Finding the Main Idea	
_____	Recalling Facts	
_____	Making Inferences	
_____	Using Words Precisely	
_____	**Reading Comprehension Score**	

Author's Approach

Put an X in the box next to the correct answer.

1. From the statements below, choose the one that you believe the author would agree with.

☐ a. Good support crews contribute to the success of the runners in the Badwater Ultramarathon.

☐ b. The Badwater Ultramarathon should be shortened for the safety of the runners.

☐ c. The Minimum Qualifying Standards for the Badwater race are too strict.

2. The author probably wrote this article in order to

☐ a. compare standard marathons to the Badwater Ultramarathon.

☐ b. persuade the reader to become a marathon runner.

☐ c. describe the challenges of the Badwater Ultramarathon.

3. What does the author imply by the statement "It is no wonder some people refer to the race as 'Satan's Fun Run'"?

☐ a. Some people call the race a fun run so it will sound easier than it really is.

☐ b. Some people think that only Satan would find the Badwater Ultramarathon fun.

☐ c. There are people who call the race "Satan's Fun Run" because they disapprove of it.

CRITICAL THINKING

4. Judging by statements from the article, you can conclude that the author wants the reader to think that

☐ a. no one should run in the Badwater Ultramarathon because the only award is a belt buckle.

☐ b. the health risks associated with ultramarathons make running in them too risky.

☐ c. the runners in the Badwater Ultramarathon are incredibly tough, motivated people.

_____ Number of correct answers

Record your personal assessment of your work on the Critical Thinking Chart on page 150.

Summarizing and Paraphrasing

Put an X in the box next to the correct answer for questions 1 and 3. Follow the directions provided for question 2.

1. Read the statement about the article below. Then read the paraphrase of that statement. Choose the reason that best tells why the paraphrase does not say the same thing as the statement.

Statement: Despite the superhuman demands of the Badwater Ultramarathon, it attracts adventure racers from around the world.

Paraphrase: Even though the Badwater Ultramarathon is tough, it attracts runners.

☐ a. Paraphrase says too much.

☐ b. Paraphrase doesn't say enough.

☐ c. Paraphrase doesn't agree with the statement.

2. Look for the important ideas and events in paragraphs 7 and 8. Summarize those paragraphs in one or two sentences.

_____

_____

_____

_____

3. Choose the sentence that correctly restates the following sentence: "Tamati did finish, and since her time was 37 hours and 14 minutes, she walked away with her very own Badwater belt buckle."

☐ a. Although it took her more than 37 hours, Tamati, who had a Badwater belt buckle, walked to the finish of the race.

☐ b. Tamati, who walked for 37 hours and 14 minutes, finished the race with her own Badwater belt buckle.

☐ c. Because Tamati finished the race in 37 hours and 14 minutes, she was awarded a Badwater belt buckle.

_____ Number of correct answers

Record your personal assessment of your work on the Critical Thinking Chart on page 150.

Critical Thinking

Put an X in the box next to the correct answer for questions 1, 2, 4, and 5. Follow the directions provided for question 3.

1. Which of the following statements from the article is an opinion rather than a fact?

☐ a. "The desert heat of the Badwater Ultramarathon is notorious for causing dehydration."

☐ b. "Major city marathons such as Boston and New York attract tens of thousands of runners every year."

☐ c. "We are built to run, to cover great distance, for survival's sake."

CRITICAL THINKING

2. From the information in paragraph 5, you can predict that

☐ a. people will apply to run in the Badwater Ultramarathon for the health benefits it offers.

☐ b. racers will continue to run for the sense of accomplishment rather than money.

☐ c. organizers will start awarding six-figure checks to the race's finishers.

3. Choose from the letters below to correctly complete the following statement. Write the letters on the lines.

In the article, _____ and _____ are different.

a. standard marathons

b. marathon runners

c. ultramarathons

4. Of the following theme categories, which would this story fit into?

☐ a. Extreme Sports

☐ b. Nature

☐ c. The American Dream

5. From the information in paragraph 8, you can conclude that

☐ a. support crew members are former marathon runners.

☐ b. having a reliable support crew could mean the difference between finishing the race and giving up.

☐ c. support crew members have medical training.

_____ Number of correct answers

Record your personal assessment of your work on the Critical Thinking Chart on page 150.

Personal Response

What was most surprising or interesting to you about this article?

_____

_____

_____

_____

Self-Assessment

Before reading this article, I already knew

_____

_____

_____

_____

_____

_____

_____

_____

_____

_____

CRITICAL THINKING

Compare and Contrast

Think about the articles you have read in Unit Three. Choose three adventures you thought were the most daring. Write the titles of the articles in the first column of the chart below. Use information you learned from the articles to fill in the empty boxes in the chart.

Title	What changes happened or were made during the adventure or journey?	How did the trailblazer act or react to the changes that occurred?	In what way did the trailblazer show creative thinking?

What is an adventure you would like to try someday? _____ What would you do to plan and

prepare for your adventure? _____

_____

_____ .

Words-per-Minute Table

Unit Three

Directions If you were timed while reading an article, refer to the Reading Time you recorded in the box at the end of the article. Use this words-per-minute table to determine your reading speed for that article. Then plot your reading speed on the graph on page 148.

Lesson	11	12	13	14	15	
No. of Words	1119	1000	1197	1129	1179	
1:30	746	667	798	753	786	90
1:40	671	600	718	677	707	100
1:50	610	545	653	616	643	110
2:00	560	500	599	565	590	120
2:10	516	462	552	521	544	130
2:20	480	429	513	484	505	140
2:30	448	400	479	452	472	150
2:40	420	375	449	423	442	160
2:50	395	353	422	398	416	170
3:00	373	333	399	376	393	180
3:10	353	316	378	357	372	190
3:20	336	300	359	339	354	200
3:30	320	286	342	323	337	210
3:40	305	273	326	308	322	220
3:50	292	261	312	295	308	230
4:00	280	250	299	282	295	240
4:10	269	240	287	271	283	250
4:20	258	231	276	261	272	260
4:30	249	222	266	251	262	270
4:40	240	214	257	242	253	280
4:50	232	207	248	234	244	290
5:00	224	200	239	226	236	300
5:10	217	194	232	219	228	310
5:20	210	188	224	212	221	320
5:30	203	182	218	205	214	330
5:40	197	176	211	199	208	340
5:50	192	171	205	194	202	350
6:00	187	167	200	188	197	360
6:10	181	162	194	183	191	370
6:20	177	158	189	178	186	380
6:30	172	154	184	174	181	390
6:40	168	150	180	169	177	400
6:50	164	146	175	165	173	410
7:00	160	143	171	161	168	420
7:10	156	140	167	158	165	430
7:20	153	136	163	154	161	440
7:30	149	133	160	151	157	450
7:40	146	130	156	147	154	460
7:50	143	128	153	144	151	470
8:00	140	125	150	141	147	480

Minutes and Seconds — Seconds

Plotting Your Progress: Reading Speed

Unit Three

Directions If you were timed while reading an article, write your words-per-minute rate for that article in the box under the number of the lesson. Then plot your reading speed on the graph by putting a small X on the line directly above the number of the lesson, across from the number of words per minute you read. As you mark your speed for each lesson, graph your progress by drawing a line to connect the Xs.

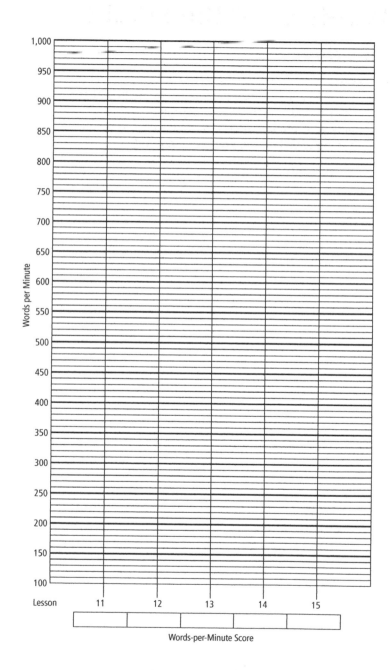

Words per Minute

Lesson   11   12   13   14   15

Words-per-Minute Score

Plotting Your Progress: Reading Comprehension

Unit Three

Directions Write your Reading Comprehension score for each lesson in the box under the number of the lesson. Then plot your score on the graph by putting a small X on the line directly above the number of the lesson and across from the score you earned. As you mark your score for each lesson, graph your progress by drawing a line to connect the Xs.

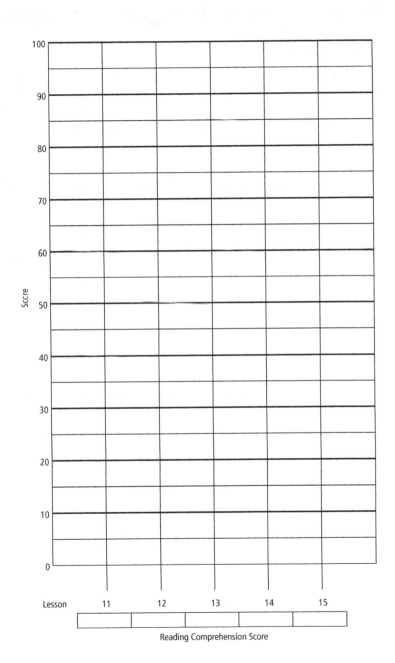

150

Plotting Your Progress: Critical Thinking

Unit Three

Directions Work with your teacher to evaluate your responses to the Critical Thinking questions for each lesson. Then fill in the appropriate spaces in the chart below. For each lesson and each type of Critical Thinking question, do the following: Mark a minus sign (–) in the box to indicate areas in which you feel you could improve. Mark a plus sign (+) to indicate areas in which you feel you did well. Mark a minus-slash-plus sign (–/+) to indicate areas in which you had mixed success. Then write any comments you have about your performance, including ideas for improvement.

Lesson	Author's Approach	Summarizing and Paraphrasing	Critical Thinking
11			
12			
13			
14			
15			